I Am. abandoned

I Am. abandoned

Blaire LaClare Koop

Demented Studios

Contents

Contents

Contents

ACKNOWLEDGEMENTS

ACKNOWLEDGEMENTS

To *John* who I am amazed by. I wouldn't have survived these last five years without you.

To Avery, my *'Beautiful boy'*; Austin, *you know that 'Everything I do I do it for you' and* Elle: you sing the song of my heart and I sing *'Your Song'*

To the rest of my family -especially you dad

ENDORESEMENTS

ENDORSEMENTS

"Blaire LaClare's "Abandoned" explores the challenges of faith within the context of medical misdiagnoses, weaving together painful childhood memories, beautiful poetry, and scriptural interpretation from her more mature point of view as a wife and mother."

"For believers, LaClare's work will serve as an inspiration, and an affirmation of their faith.

"However, atheists like me will be left frustrated, hoping LaClare will continue to honestly and skeptically self-reflect, and consider the possibility that she, and not some supernatural entity, did the emotional labour that brought her to the place so beautifully described in her narrative."

-Christine Shellska, phD candidate at the University of Calgary

****

You will come away changed. The honesty and transparency that Blaire tells her story with will grip and captivate you. Through the challenges and difficulties of hopelessness, rejection and heartbreak, she has persevered and is found still standing, writing the next chapters of her story on her own terms. With courage, humour and strength, Blair shares with us some of her battle with mental and physical illness). You are sure to be inspired .

-Tracy Lenko, Associate Pastor, 4 Square Mission, Saskatchewan

COPYRIGHT

ISBN 13: 978-17777705-2-5
Ebook 978-17777705-1-8

For worldwide distribution, printed in the USA

CRUSHED

The sound was like thunder,
The crumbling of your heart.
I'm all to blame.
I've never hurt anyone's soul
Until now.
The feelings hurts
More than you can imagine.
I hold out my hand again
But my fingers go limp
Against my side.
You don't know you have
a good thing until it's gone.
I broke your heart
But you took mine with you too.
I am crushed.
The sun hurts my eyes
Because brightness is so unlike
My soul.
I only know foolishness
And loss.

If I wouldn't have acted
On my notions
I would smile at
The sun. and at you.

SECTION 1: STOP THE DRAMA DIVA DEE DEE

I liked soccer quite a lot but it was never a great passion. I was also a forward in hockey but I always sucked- and I was not crazy about playing.

When I was about 14 I became –I forget how this happened- the goalie of my girls' hockey team; I actually quite liked it but I was scared of open spaces so the ice wasn't often my friend.

But there was one thing that was my forte, one sport that seemed to choose me more than I chose it, and when it did, I never looked back. I felt it was part of who I was and I couldn't be without it. Since I thought it was my identity, if I failed at it, I would have failed myself.

****

CHAPTER 1

Drama: I absolutely loved it and was good at it. I loved the other, older actors; I loved learning lines; I loved speaking loudly; I loved drama festival. Despite everything that was happening in my current real life, stepping on that stage for the 1st three years calmed me and made me feel safe.

-

My first year of drama -grade 7- was bright and shiny and awe-ful and new. This was a talent I never knew I had; this was something I had never imagined. Drama calmed me and kept me in rapture- 'attacks' weren't even a thought when I was doing drama.

I loved my next role even better: an 8-year-old boy named Benjamin in a play called 'The Yellow Boat'. He had hemophilia and AIDS; a stretch to play, for sure, but a challenge I met with head on! The directors had made an actual, life-sized, plywood yellow boat that I got to sit on- this made spaces non-threatening. Also, I had to concentrate in order to fit the role of a sick little boy. How could I have had -or even thought of- 'attacks' then?

In grade nine I played a snobby, trouble causing girl from the 70s; I twirled my hair, jived and had an amazing time. I found it a little bit of an outlet. In real life I wanted to not be scared and to be a care-free, pack-leading girlie-girl; this I became onstage. I rarely worried about open spaces which would have likely triggered intense fear which would have triggered the 'things.'

7

So what about grade 10? That year's character was a middle-aged spinster named Hester; a character whose father died years earlier but she still mourned grievously. She and her brother live in their dad's house. She feels she needs the house to keep her father's memory alive.

That is why, when her brother and new wife want to sell the house, she murders them. She thinks the murder will protect her, not seeing how vulnerable she really is. She loses her brother in order to control what she can't. She is so sick that she can't see that she is living a totally surreal, horrid life.

That's where my sickness came in. Playing nervous Hester required me -obviously- to act nervous. *Acting* nervous made me *become* nervous. Since *being nervous* was a trigger for my 'attacks', I was not calm like other years.

That year, I was aware of fears, was anxious, and soured a little of what I loved -drama- in the process. I, like Hester, lost part of me in my pain.

***

The Drama Festival in grade 10 took place in St. Walburg. A different school hosted Drama Festival every year and it was their turn. We arrived in St. Walburg on a Thursday; we were going to spend the day watching other school's plays and going to some workshops. Friday morning was our performance. I figured almost immediately that *that* day would not be any easy one. My seizures or attacks or whatever they were, were getting bad.

Though St. Walburg was not far from Edam, I was not well acquainted with the town or the school. And why did that matter? Because I always needed to have the advantage of knowing the lay-out so that I could make a battle plan in my mind- and everything was a battle just to 'get through.' How was I to figure out what to do to appear sane and even feel that way a little tiny bit, if I didn't know where to go to make these things happen? I wasn't exited for that year's drama... not really anyway.

I had always loved the acting workshops that were interesting and made me feel like part of something instead of just the weird girl that fell, alone, convulsing on the floor. I also was usually thrilled as the idea of performing; yes, it was nerve wracking, especially when my part was huge like it was with Benjamin the 8 year old hemophiliac, but it was always exhilarating none-the-less.

Then there was the camaraderie: being with kids of different ages -because as you might know, drama, especially small town school drama, includes a group of actors from all age groups in grade 7 to 12. I should have been anticipating only fun times but instead I was anticipating imminent disaster.

*

My drama group put our bags in our designated classroom-to-be-bedroom. Mrs. Young and Mrs. Sideroff then herded us to our workshop which was in some hard-to-get to location in the school. It required us to leave the side doors, go around the outside, back in the front entrance and down a hallway; I thought that it was the weirdest set-up in the world... and I was terrified.

I stayed very extremely close to a girl named Christine. I talked to her the whole way while walking backwards so I could distract myself from the open space we were in. Finally we neared the front entrance doors; I was beyond relieved. It really seemed like I was going to make it.

Suddenly Christine heard the end of something that two other girls were saying. She turned and walked back to them. No one stood right next to me and I freaked out. With only self-preservation in mind I grabbed onto the nearest person - Mrs. Young.

"Are you alright Blaire?" she awkwardly and with mortification, asked me while looking sideways at Mrs. Sideroff for help. Every single fear that I'd harbored that day came rushing out of me un-hindered.

I didn't care about the fact that I was embarrassing myself in front of people that I wanted to impress. I didn't care about any-thing but feeling safe. When you're afraid -like really, really afraid-everything else pales in comparison.

"I am not okay Mrs. Young!" I shouted in a horrified voice that surely everyone present heard. "You're not coming down with the flu this weekend of all weekends?" Mrs. Young queried. "No, I just cannot walk into that hallway and into that room!" "Do you not like the adjudicator?" she asked, still oblivious to what was happening in my head and body.

"No," I said still much too loudly, "I just can't go in! I just can't do it!" I was very near tears. Mrs. Sideroff, who knew me better and also was generally calmer, stepped in. She told the rest of the Edam kids to go inside and said casually, "Mrs. Young and I will stay out-side with Blaire for a moment." The cast and crew looked at us very oddly but left.

Then Mrs. Sideroff turned to Judy Young and me. She gently took my arms from Mrs. Young's and held me in a half hug. She told Mrs. Young to go into the classroom with all the rest of the actors and the adjudicator. She looked relieved to not have to be in the porch (where we now were) with me freaking out.

"Okay," Mrs. Sideroff began kindly once the door had been closed, "what is wrong Blaire?"

"Well didn't you hear me tell Mrs. Young?" I said weakly. "I heard what you said," Mrs. Sideroff began slowly and carefully lest she said something that upset me further.

She continued, "The thing is that I don't understand. What are you scared of?" I do not know if my explanation helped Mrs. Sideroff as much as it probably confused her, but I spilled: "I have seizures but the neurologist doctors don't think I have seizures.

They told me that I have something screwed up in my head and that they can't treat me and all they did is sticking me on some pills.

"But the pills don't help me and sending me to psychiatrists that can't treat me because I, like, know I have seizures but the neurologist doctors say I'm wrong all the time.

"But in a way I have something wrong with my head because I have an aphobia" -at that time I seriously thought that it was actually one word long- "that has something to do with the seizures maybe. And the seizures make me scared or having an aphobia makes me have seizures or something like that.

"But then more often I'm really sure that then since I see all these psychiatrists who give me relaxation tapes and tell me I have anxiety and an aphobia of open spaces, I started getting a phobia of open spaces."

Mrs. Sideroff, trying to understand the last sentence or so, reiterated what I'd said, "So you're saying that you are anxious and you have a phobia and that you were scared because you were in an open space?" I kind of nodded. By that time, she'd coaxed me into the boot room, just inside the school doors. She continued,

"Okay, so you are just anxious because of the open spaces. So if I we sit down for a few minutes and talk before entering the room everything should be ok?" "No, everything wouldn't be okay because I don't just have attacks, I have maybe 'pseudo-seizures' and no one listens to me, especially God." I said all of it, but especially the last part, full of bitterness.

"What will happen if I go into the open hallway is that my scaredness will probably get so bad that I have a 'seizure' and, like, a 'seizure' for me, is really bad because it doesn't hurt but they scare me.

"If I have a 'seizure' the right side of my body shakes and my face freezes and I can hear and see you but I can't talk to you and then I fall down usually because my leg won't hold me up and during an attack my left leg is useless to help me stand up and then that's embarrassing."

Trying to help me and not hurt me more she said, "If an attack doesn't hurt you, and if it really doesn't matter if I see because I would never make fun of you and you don't need to feel embarrassment then is it really so bad. After all, you became very afraid near the entrance to the school, where our entire group and other school children could hear you. This would probably not be as bad." She had a very valid point but I didn't agree anyway. In a pitiful voice I just mumbled out, "No matter what, I'd be really scared and embarrassed."

Mrs. Sideroff was going to get me a chair to sit in when the 'seizure' came on. As soon as it was over I got to my feet without any sort of assistance and brushed off my pants. I didn't want any fussing over me or my 'attack.' I just wanted to be normal. My 'post-attack' actions were entirely different than they were just moments earlier. I stoically said, "Okay, I'm ready to go into the workshop. Coming?"

My outside appearance was fairly collected but inside I was truly a horrible mess. Mrs. Sideroff was obviously confused. She started to ask if I was okay or a zillion of other things, but since I didn't answer, she just walked behind me; we were both lost in our own thoughts.

Once in the room I behaved as if nothing had happened though the whole entire rest of the day I was detached and inwardly embarrassed.

***

On Friday morning I got out of my sleeping bag before anyone else was up and walked quietly to the bathroom. My fear was not monumental (I jumped from desk to desk and then hung on the door to gain composure before entering the bathroom, so for me it was okay).

When I exited a few minutes later I was relatively calm. True, I found several other girls awake. This made me more self-conscious on the walk back but I remained upright and 'attack-less.' All things considered, Friday started out really well and I was a little bit hopeful.

When it came to breakfast at the cafeteria, I stayed close to Lyndsey. She was in my grade at school and though she may not have understood my antics and 'peculiarities,' I sort of trusted her not to bolt and she sort of knew how to symbiotically act around me.

We got breakfast and made it safely to the table. This day was looking decently optimistic; Mrs. Young told us our itinerary for the morning. Directly after breakfast was to be our dress rehearsal; one step closer to performing. I began to be quite nervous- not so much for performing as for having to be scared in front of other people (try to make sense of that nuance).

The optimism I'd had only moments before was waning greatly and very quickly.

*

The props were in the box of Mrs. Young's truck. The older, stronger kids in our group loaded them into the gym and onto the stage. Backstage, I dressed in my simple costume – plain cotton, long sleeved dress and slippers.

I was careful not to wreck my hair- it had been coiffed and sprinkled with almost an entire bottle of baby powder. I grabbed the black Holy Bible that I was to carry with me onstage and felt a lot of anxiety coming on.

Transferring from one position to another was often terrifying and nearly impossible. In this instance going to the wings where I was to start the play at stage right was a horrible ordeal but I managed it. Though I didn't die… or even anything less dramatic as that, such as having an attack, I was shaken.

And I became very aware that I would soon have to move from the wing onto the stage.

I stood there, petrified and feeling completely alone, despite the presence of Brandon (aka Hester's brother) and Christine (sister-in-law) who were also waiting.

Breaking through my horrid thoughts, Mrs. Young prompted, "Ready guys?" and I fell apart. The Bible fell from my hands and onto the floor. My right leg began shaking, soon my right arm did too and then half my face became numb.

As I fell to the stage floor I caught a glance at Mrs. Young and Mrs. Sideroff below: the horrified looks that passed between them. I felt their certain expectation that I would collapse on stage. The anticipation of my imminent ruin of everything they had worked months for engulfed my mind.

When it was over I saw Christine covering her eyes with her hands, near tears. She was saying, "Oh my g**, oh my g**," over and over. *I* thought my *life* was absolutely over.

In *my* life, very little was as important to me as drama; I was good at something and I loved being recognized for it. The rest of the time my whole being seemed to revolve around my weirdness and my problems.

Having the directors disappointed in me was torture. Thinking that they were thinking that I was not fit to act was almost the worst thing ever. It was the lowest I felt that entire year. It may have been the biggest disappointment in my life since the 'attacks' began.

Then Brandon nonchalantly asked if he could help me up. He and I didn't always see eye to eye (probably because I felt he stole my limelight because he was a pretty good actor). But I think his nonchalant demeanor at that moment was the only thing that helped me say, "Okay, moving on."

*

As it turned out I did *not* have a 'seizure' during our performance. I was relieved but I was not joyful as one might have expected. The excitement of a play well-done usually was all-encompassing for at least a few minutes. That year, while everyone was congratulating each other and beaming, I quietly sat down with my thoughts.

I'd never felt more abandoned than then.

CHAPTER 2

Every year, one week before drama *festival*, we held a drama *community* night. When that night came, I was very excited but as always, a little nervous. Also as always, I was not so much nervous about the performance –being on stage and the time before of being in the gym knowing that people were anticipating our play- but I was nervous about how I could get around.

While still at home getting ready for going to drama community night, I wracked my brain for something to ease my anxiety. The first idea that popped into my head was to carry something with me so I didn't feel like I was so alone or that open spaces were as open.

I looked around the porch that I was in waiting for mom to be ready, and the first my eyes alighted on was an old pillow that someone had left laying against the wall there. I grabbed the big soft old thing and relished in the tiny bit of protection I believed it gave me.

Even in the midst of my relief, I knew what I was doing was insane but did it seem worth it? Yes it did.

God protected me. God protects me. God says that the angel of the Lord encamps around those who love him and

16

saves them. I didn't know that verse then though. And even
had I known that verse I would have found a million reasons
to not think it applied to me.

God might not stop the seizure/attack/issue but He promises to be with us. There might be a reason we say we go
'through' problems; we are not meant to stay there or even go
around.

If you are busy having your eyes on Jesus, your problems
don't seem so monumental. And while the problems seem like
a reflection on yourself, they won't so much. When you let
yourself know how much God is for you- as weird as it is- the
physical failings don't feel so bad.

I heard mom yell that she would be out in just a minute so I
knew I had to head out to the car to go to the school. I crept around
things in our yard, got to the car, opened the door and climbed in
the backseat.

Fabian, sitting up front, looked from me and to the pillow and
back again, clearly wanting to say something. He waited a few
moments for effect and then sarcastically asked, "What insane thing
are you doing now Blaire? Does this have anything to do with
your 'wacko' syndrome?" I said nothing. He was a little jerk, but he
was right.

A few minutes later mom got in the car and pulled out of our
driveway; neither Fabian nor I mentioned the pillow. Neither mom
nor Nikki (who had climbed in the back on the driver's side and
now sat only a foot from me in the dark car) had a chance to see the
pillow because I had it crammed with me in the backseat.

I knew they would notice when I had to get out of the car but I tried to ignore that inevitability. When mom parked in the school lot, I got out and pulled my pillow along with me.

Mom looked over, saw me and sighed dramatically, "What on earth are you doing Blaire?" "Mom, this pillow is going"- I said while continuing towards the doors- "to help me so I have to take it with me, that's all." Had anyone been watching my face, they would have seen me wipe away a tear.

To my back mom shouted, "Blaire, you have got to get over this and stop it! You can't take a pillow in with you to the dessert theatre, we'll all look insane!"

I stopped in my tracks and snapped my head –with the pillow still in my arms- towards mom, "Is that all you care about mom, how everything will make *you* look? Well, like, I have some new information for you: You're not very nice at all!

"I know that I am a freakin' nutcase, thinking that a pillow is going to help me when we all know that God hates me and nothing is going to help me, but still I have come to this conclusion that I need this pillow and I will take it in with me.

"Do you think I like looking like a fool in front of, like, all these people? No, I don't, and if I had any choice in the matter I would leave the pillow in the car.

"But the fact is that I will embarrass myself if I take the pillow in with me and I'll embarrass myself even more if I have a seizure and fall on the floor. This isn't to mention the fact that I'll feel terrified if I have to go in there with nothing with me so just you never mind."

Mom just shook her head, sighed and walked up behind me. She gently put her hand on my shoulder.She said, "Blaire, God is with you so you don't have be afraid ... and I am with you too, you don't need your pillow.

"And for what you said about being embarrassed, how do you possibly think it's more embarrassing to have a little 'attack' on the floor than it is if you carry a pillow to the gym?" I just said, "Whatever," and walked in.

*

The first person that I saw was a girl named Ashley K. She was one of the students serving the desserts that night. She came up to me and grabbed the edge of my pillow: "Blaire, what's this for?" I thought hard and then lied, "Um, I have the pillow with me, like, because it's a prop for the play."

Ashely's face and words belied her disbelief: "I thought that all of the props would be ready backstage already and that you wouldn't have to bring your... um... pillow from home, that's all."

'Why is she bugging me for specifics about my pillow?' I thought, 'Just let me go so I don't have to stand in the boot lobby, feeling uncomfortable.'

Before she could continue our wonderful conversation I said with strained pleasantness "I have to get in there and see if they have pistachio pie here, see you later Ashely!" I ran into the gym before I could be scared. Or see the confused look on her face.

With my pillow in hand, I stood just inside the gym, surveying. It took a minute in the dim lighting but I spotted Danielle. My face lit up and pillow in hand I walked to her. I said without preamble, "Hi Danielle," I said, "What kinds of pie do they all have? And when are we on?"

Not looking up at me and not seeing my pillow, she was used to my random questions and began to answer in order. She explained, "There's a lot here and we won't get much time to eat because we have to get backstage pretty soon to get ready but the teachers said us drama kids can eat as many left overs as we want.

Then she leaned closer to me to rearrange a pie plate and saw my pillow. With narrowed eyes she said, "Blaire, come on now, get a grip on reality! You know that you can't carry that around with you! Man, when I'm done here you can stand beside me and calm your nerves or whatever you think you have to do but for Pete's sake, leave the pillow under the table or in the change room or something less embarrassing!"

"So you know then, hey?" I asked. "Of course I know what you're doing!" she retorted. Sheepishly I asked, "So, you wouldn't believe me if I said that the pillow is just a prop?" I asked awkwardly. "No I wouldn't believe you Blaire, I know you!"

Then she did me a huge favor (although I never thought so at the time). She grabbed the pillow out of my hand before I had any time to stop her. I started to say, "Danielle, what are you doing?" Before I got all the words out, my lips froze and I felt my right arm and leg go numb.

With my left hand I clenched onto the table. I grabbed a raspberry cheesecake which crashed to the floor. A nearby teacher asked, "Blaire, what is happening?" Try as I might, I could not answer (although, uncharacteristically, I was still standing upright).

When the 15 second 'attack' was over I looked over at the teacher. She was by then on the ground, picking up the cake and looked at me, "Blaire, what were you doing? Didn't you notice that you had dropped the cake?"

I was very grateful for the semi-dark room that partially hid my face from the teacher.

Telling the truth seemed like the worst idea ever so I said the first thing that came to my mind: "Um, I hurt my knee in gym class today and then when I went to look at the table I bumped my knee and hurt it and a huge jolt of pain run up it.

"My knee was kind of, like, paralyzed for a minute but now it's okay and um... here, let me go throw that in the garbage." She just mumbled, "Um, sure, there's one over there."

I knew that something was stopping God from helping me

and it made me mad because I thought that I deserved help. One problem was that my idea of help was a little different than His and I valued mine the most.

I wanted Him to take every problem away while He wanted me to learn to love Him unconditionally. So until I got the help I wanted, I thought that I was justified in continuing on in my same routine. Fear, anxiety and not obeying or having faith in Him seemed justified until He fulfilled my expectations.

I should have been saying "I will praise You in this storm" and "abase me or abound me, whatever but I am yours."

Instead I said, "I'll praise You if You do what I want.

CHAPTER 3

Ms. Formanek had been my drama coach when I'd won the Mary Ellen Burgess Award for excellence in acting; we had formed a bond. It was through her that in September 1997 -grade 9- that I heard about the community theatre to place in Cochin (a small town nearby).

I thought it must be something nearly as prestigious as Hollywood. My young mind filled with thoughts of something akin to the big time. Ms. Formanek said tryouts were done, but she knew the director and could get me an audition.

I was absolutely beside myself with excitement!

***

The audition was an hour away at an Anglican church in North Battleford. Mom drove and Danielle came along for emotional support. As much as her presence calmed me, my anxiety in my anticipation of entering the church increased every second.

By the time we pulled up to the parking lot across the street from the church the apprehension was insane. Not the apprehension of performing, but the realization that everything was a scary space that I had to navigate through.

When we arrived, Danielle asked if she should come in with me. I said yes, of course. Danielle was my best friend and so much more than just some tactic to get through my sick little life. But I fully admit that at that moment, I needed her there so I could survive: crossing the street, walking up the stairs and through the door....

Danielle helped me get inside the building but for the audition itself, I was on my own. At the door to the audition room, she patted me on the back (I think she was fully aware of how terrified I was) and said, "I'll wait in the hallway. I'm sure you'll be great."

I stood there in the open door for a second with Danielle motioning me to breathe and go inside. When I finally opened the door, I was acutely aware that there were several chairs in the room and that none of them were near me. They wouldn't help me get from the doors to the director's table and then to the stage 10 feet away.

On seeing me walk in the door, the director slid out of his chair and turned towards me. He cooed, "Aah, you must be Blaire, how are you?" Every nerve in my body was doing jumping jacks. I awkwardly and too loudly said, "I'm rearing and ready to go!"

"Well, I'm glad to hear you're eager, I'd really love to see you in action, especially after what Patti –I guess that would be Ms. Formanek to you- said." I wanted to ask what she'd said but I was almost sick thinking of how to get to the stage and didn't bother. "By the way, my name is Bill," the man said pleasantly.

I feigned interest though inside I was dying of anxiety. "Yeah," I said very nervously, "and my name is Blaire." I immediately regretted my words because I knew that of course Bill knew my name. While I didn't appreciate sounding like a fool, it didn't bother me that much. I had bigger fish to fry... all of the time.

I stood by the doors for a few awkward seconds in which Bill just waited for me, wondering what I was doing. Finally I took a deep breath and held it. I dug the fingernails of my right hand into my right arm until I could actually see blood come to the surface of my skin and then I skipped to the table.

Bill was a little taken aback, and a look of, 'is she insane?' crossed his face. My consideration of his assessment of me was short lived. I was more preoccupied with noting I had made it intact to the table. I said, "Oh hi Bill," because I was so flustered.

Bill awkwardly said, "Um, well I guess I should tell you about the part." He gestured to the stage and said, "Well, why don't you get up on the stage." I closed my eyes because the stage was several feet away, ran to the stage and swung myself up.

Once on the stage I panicked. Blood seemed to rush through every artery in my body and then erupt in my ears. I couldn't hear anything but the nearly audible thrumming of, 'you're terrified, you're terrified, you're terrified.'

Bill was talking about the play but I only heard segments of what he said. The words, "Well I guess that is it, so now if you could, I would like you to begin reading…" somehow broke through my crazy.

What were the other things he had said? The stress was overcoming me. Willing to do nearly anything to ease the pressure, I shoved my hand in my mouth. Seriously, almost my whole hand.

I knew I had to explain and explain quickly. Stuttering and stumbling I said, "Um, my hand was terribly itchy and I tried to not, like, freak because it was so itchy but then I just had to scratch it so, um, like, I put it in my mouth." Then I laughed awkwardly.

Bill did not acknowledge the hand-biting or the explanation. In reality, I don't think he had a clue what to say. In a voice that did little to hide his annoyance and incredulity, he repeated himself. When I looked stunned and confused (because I'd missed almost all of his directions while thinking of open spaces and battle plans to help me get through the time in the building) he said with an almost audible sigh, "The part of the teenage girl."

Leaning over to take the script from his hand nearly threw me into an 'attack'. Innately wanting to do anything to stop it, I roughly fell down into the small couch behind me. I got up very quickly it was too late to stop him from thinking I was a loon.

"Okay then," I said while he looked mildly troubled "I guess I'm going to read the part to you now." Bill may have found this whole scenario odd, but he thought that I had nothing more than acting jitters. He soothed, "Just relax Blaire." Very uncertainly I replied, "Right."

Reading the lines I queried, "What is it that you would like me to do mother?" but I only got as far as "...like me...?" before I lunged at the stage's prop door on my left. Bill looked at me in shock, daring me with his eyes to come up with some sort of plausible explanation.I lunged back to my original position and said, "Oh, mother, I was just pushing the door to keep out the draft because I figured that you would like me to."

He raised his hands to say, 'audition over'. I finished off my crazy act by grabbing the skin of my hips and pulling on it. Bill said, "Blaire, I've seen enough. You can be done." He stood and muttered, "I will get back to Ms. Formanek," and that was all.

I nodded numbly, knowing what that decision would be. I'd improvised a weird rap routine in the short time I was onstage. Before that I had skipped and catapulted, and I would have to do it all over again on the way out. My Cochin acting career was not looking bright.

***

It was the school hallway a week later, during one of our short recesses. I was surrounded by my classmates; I quite relished how close and congested everything was.

I had a hard time seeing anyone specific in the blur, but then Ms. Formanek appeared. She wore an emotion that I judged to be somewhere between sadness and disappointment- I knew exactly what was coming.

She pushed past all the other kids until she was in front of me.

My eyes blocked out everyone except her. I read everything in her look to say, "You are not awesome and our bond isn't either."

Without preamble she said, "I talked to Bill." I knew what the answer would be before I asked it and yet I said, "What did Bill have to say Ms. Formanek?"

A moment went by but it seemed like an eternity. Finally she put her hand on my shoulder (and Ms. Formanek is not a touchy-feely, soft kind of lady)."Blaire, he didn't think you were right for the part." She kind of searched my face an explanation for what Bill had obviously told her. I faux smiled and said, "Maybe next time!"

We both knew, though, that there was no 'next time.' In my head I heard her shout, 'You blew it, I don't know what you did but you blew it. I am sad at this moment in time. I am disappointed in you.' *I* was also very sad at that moment.

But the embarrassment didn't end with Ms. Formanek turning her back on me and walking away. Most of the girls in my class had heard –since before the audition- that I was trying out. They were slightly amused and my 'screw up' when I considered myself such an actor.

Being on stage was a refuge for me, a time to forget my fears at least a little bit. Usually I was just thought of as being the sick weird girl, but when I acted people seemed impressed. I felt that I had near-fatally wounded so much more than a hobby. It was truly one of the worst slaps in the face I couldn't have imagined.

CHAPTER 4

Going into grade 7 and nearing the end of the century -1995, whoa- I had had great expectations.

I was going to be in high school (in Edam, we only have one school that houses kindergarten to grade 12). We got to change classes and not have the same teacher all the time. We would have our own lockers. It was good.

Then I got to grade 7 and found out that the perks were far less than the drawbacks. We couldn't play soccer, changing classes wasn't that exciting, lockers were just like the desks we had in elementary and all the teachers seemed as sucky as before.

I was desperate for something to break up the mundanity. When I heard, about 6 weeks into school, about drama try-out at lunch a few days from now, I was in like a dirty shirt. I knew little about acting and I wasn't terribly interested in it, but anything possibly not monotonous was welcomed.

***

One other grade 7 kid went to tryouts: Aaron. Other than that, the kindergarten room where try-outs were held was full of big, seemingly mature, confidant and skilled youths whom, for the most part, I didn't know. I was very intimidated.

Try-outs consisted of jumping around and acting like a pirate. People all over were putting their hands up to their faces like they were looking out from a huge sailing ship over some unseen horizon. I had no idea what to do so I just copied them. I was sure, though, that I was totally horrible at it.

When try-outs were over I felt very disappointed in myself, which kind of surprised me since I had suddenly started to like it. I had decided that I loved acting and now I would never get to do because of my lack of skills.

So Aaron and I were about to walk out of the room when Mrs. Young, one of the directors, beckoned us. Smiling, she said, "Blaire and Aaron, you got the part!" "What?" we both asked because she seemed to make no sense.

"Well, you didn't *both* get it I guess. You both did wonderful at try-outs. Mrs. Sideroff" -she gestured at the other drama director- "and I both thought so. The only problem," Mrs. Young began, "is that we are not sure which one of you to give the part of Clown to."

Mrs. Sideroff spoke up, "Well, maybe there's someone in grade one who hasn't went for recess yet, let's see if any of the kids are left in the room." On checking, a grade 1 boy named Jordan was and he looked a little taken off guard by two teachers saying they wanted to speak to him.

"Jordan, this is Blaire and Aaron," Mrs. Sideroff gestured at the two of us. "We need you to break a tie between these two. I've put both their names in a hat. Whoever you pick will be the one who wins." Jordan looked nervous but came forward, mixed the names around in the hat and then picked one.

"Blaire?" Jordan said with a bit of a question in his voice. "Seriously?" I asked, trying to sound extremely nonchalant, but I wore a little smile on my face. Aaron just shrugged his shoulders like he really didn't care and said, "Congratulations Blaire."

"Yeah, you did a good job too Aaron," I offered as a polite side-note.

IT

in It's life span
time is No factor. It
is a Monster to
Be rid of. But you Can't.
It lurks in the shadows
of your mind.
just when you think
you've Overcome It
It attacks you and
it hurts you so bad you
wish Death upon
yourself.
what else can you do?
you've tried everything there
Is. Your mind
Is clouded by It. It
casts shadows like
clouds and Blocks out
all sunshine.
Nothing can grow. and you

cry. but tears don't help,
clouds love rain, your cloud
loves tears. and Thrives on
Them.
No one to run to,
No one really cares,
Their faux sympathy
Insults you and makes you cringe.
The sun shines brightly upon
Their lives. What do they fear.
Things normal people fear?
Not like you. Yours is real. There. It lives
in you . In the inner depths
Of your Mind.
It is King. You are
It's Slave
Pick yourself up off
The ground. You once were Master,
Ruler. Till It came along.
You were weak. It
Overcame you. Engulfed.
Fight! For once in your
Pathetic Existence Fight!
Or do you Want to stay
Prisoner in your Own
Home ?

SECTION 2: YOU CAN'T STOP THE BIRDIES OF SADNESS FROM FLYING OVER YOUR HEAD BUT YOU CAN STOP THEM FROM NESTING IN YOUR ATTACK

A few years ago I wrote a paper for my bachelor of psychology degree; it was titled "The Crossroads theory of nature, nurture and free-will choice on development". I've used this term many times before and it really seems to hit home.

Sometimes you feel pooped on, but you don't have to dwell, you can just wash up and move on.

Or sometimes you let the birds of sadness just move in

and you might realize that they don't make very good room-mates.

****

CHAPTER 5

Shortly after the birdy day, Ms. Gatzkin took our class on a trip to the North Battleford pool. It was a mixed joy for me. I wanted to be there doing 'normal' kid stuff and I loved the pool but I was also scared of an unfamiliar place. It was hard to make a battle plan when there were so many unknowns.

Most of the kids probably thought about getting their suits on as fast as possible and getting into the water. I just thought of every single move to get to the pool relatively unscathed. Not sure if I wanted to but not sure I wanted to stay in the lobby either, I went into the girls' change room.

It was terrible: hard, slippery floors that beckoned us to take off our socks. There was one plus I guess- the humid air that was infused with chlorine was heavier. This at least was comforting (I can't even explain how but it was). The first thing I noticed, as one might expect, was the entrance and what was there: lockers, change stalls and then benches. Around the corner there was a stall of showers. Beyond that was the swimming pool area.

Taking in the room was sensory overload. I saw and felt too much. I wanted to scream and grab onto someone but few people would ever understand or help. To make matters worse, I had somehow lost Danielle in the big, open, rough, damp place.

I felt alone and terrified. Desperate, I followed my cousin Suzanne; I pretended I wanted to be really near her to talk. Then, near the change room benches, Suzanne suddenly turned and walked back towards the door to grab something she had dropped on the floor. I was alone. I panicked and ran to the bench with my eyes closed.

Once I reached them I sat and started whistling to distract my brain from my horrendously fearful thoughts. Annoyed looks came from the other girls but at that moment, whistling calmed me; it became the lesser of two evils. I managed to get my bathing suit out of my bag. I scanned the room for a stall, whistling all the while.

A stall door opened and someone stepped out. I quickly grabbed my bag, closed my eyes and hopped and jumped to reach it. I was very aware that I looked like a complete nut. The fact I was soon feeling relatively safe enveloped in the closed quarters of the change stall made me happy, though. For a moment.

I realized that I could not stay there for long. With resolve I quickly got dressed and exited. Ms. Gatzkin got out of the stall next to me at about the same time. I was suddenly overcome with fear. I did the first thing that popped into my mind. I grabbed onto the top of the change stall doors and I hung, lifting my feet off the ground.

Ms. Gatzkin saw and said, aghast, "Blaire, are you okay? What are you doing?" I lowered my feet back to the floor, let go of the stall door and jumped to the bench. I scrunched my face, thinking, and said, "Um, I was just telling the girls earlier that I thought this door was loose and I was just, like, checking it." "Well, get off the door and... um, go sit on the changing bench till we are all ready to go out together."

Sitting on the bench, I again started thinking of how I might get safely to the pool area. I was thinking that I would feel less vulnerable with a group. 'Maybe,' I conjectured, 'No one at all would notice that I am uncomfortable and maybe I'll look cool.' Then I heard, "Okay girls, it's time to go" and all my notions melted.

Bewildered and at a loss for what to do I just yelled, "Aah!"

Everyone stopped in their tracks. I heard someone say, "Oh here we go again." Most days I would have focused on finding the person who dared insult me... but I was currently too scared to move. Ms. Gatzkin walked towards me to see what was wrong. When she got close to me I threw myself at her.

Shocked, she just stood there, stiff as a board, with a very flabbergasted look on her face. In an absolutely tortured voice I pleaded, "Please don't make me go out there, I am just too terrified!" She just stared at me. The girl that had been making fun of me moments before said, "No one understands, not even Blaire herself so don't worry about it Ms. G." I would have attacked her if I had been able to turn away from Ms. Gatzkin.

Speaking to me like I was a child, she said, "Blaire, we need to have a shower before we go to the pool, okay?" Ms. Gatzkin peeled me several inches away from her while still holding onto my wrist. Then, looking sideways she hissed, "Danielle, could you help me here?" I guess she knew we were close. Danielle flippantly retorted, "Ms. Gatzkin, all the other teachers know what to do with her, can't you take care of it yourself?" Gritting her teeth, Ms. Gatzkin hissed, "Danielle, right now please!"

I interjected, "What the heck is this? You're all talking about me while I'm standing, like, right here like I'm some kind of coma patient or something! For your information I have a disease that has nothing to do with being crazy... well, not exactly crazy, and I don't like how you're talking about me as if I'm not here!"

"I'm so sorry," Ms Gatzkin said, still bewildered; from the little I knew of Ms. Gatzkin I had gathered she was not a hugging kind of lady. That was probably why I just fell apart crying when she hugged me and tried to comfort me. Still clinging to her, my right leg started to go numb. I was convulsing but not deaf. I heard Devin say from around the corner, "what the heck are all the girls doing?"

Aaron's voice said "Blaire is...."

Devin replied, "Oh, I get it. I swear that it never stops."

CHAPTER 6

Nicolle and I were conversing about Mr. Noodle noodle cups when it started. Suddenly the toes of my right foot curled, and I stopped speaking and then I fell over –a pretty typical 'attack' and a pretty typical day. Nicolle knew what was coming too because she also stopped speaking and stuck her hands on her hips in a relaxed position. She obviously knew she wouldn't have to wait long.

It was grade 8, 1996- Ms. Gatzkin was the new Phy. Ed. teacher. While standing near her office. that day, she saw me lying on the ground, shaking, and ran over at lightning speed. Bobbi, who she'd been talking to, followed, but in more of a saunter - Bobbi had seen this many times too. When she got there she said, "She's fine Ms. Gatzkin, this happens all the time."
Ms. Gatzkin turned her head andshouted, "Does she look just fine to you Bobbi?" Bobbi replied rather blasé, "Yes, as a matter of fact I'd have to say so." Ignoring Bobbi's comments, Ms. Gatzkin crouched down to help me.While steadying my neck and looking under-statedly concerned, she probed, "Blaire? Blaire? Can you hear me?" I never answered because my face was still frozen, which freaked her out all the more.

It was only a few seconds later the 'seizure' (I used the words interchangeably because I thought they were seizures but was told they were panic attacks) was over and I was able to move. I imme-diately pushed myself back to sitting and then standing. I adjusted my hair that had become messed during my 'attack': "Now what was the score again?" Ms. Gatzkin was obviously flabbergasted at my resurrection of sorts.

She half-screeched, "Blaire, what are you talking about?" "Well we're playing badminton still, right? Or did my attack last so long that I missed that we started something else?" -the jokes I made to cover up my embarrassment were lame, but I tried. She demanded, "What the heck happened?"

I said, "Oh, it was nothing really. I just have these attacks that are actually probably seizures while I'm in the gym and in other open spaces. They don't last very long and I just shake a little and that's about all." I thought I had explained my 'attacks' quite well and logically. I was quite hopeful that the rest of class would be uneventful. I turned to Nicolle to carry on with our game but no such luck.

The encounter caught Christopher's attention which made me grimace. Christopher very rarely said anything nice to me... or even civil; he was usually a giant jerk (well, I was no better to him either). He generally led the pack in saying my attacks/seizures were just part of my 'lying-diva-in-need-of-attention' act. Needless to say, he wasn't on my 'star friends list.' Without being invited to weigh in on the matter, he sarcastically said, "And then she can't talk but that's okay because it gives the rest of us a break from listening to her babble." I wanted to grab Christopher and kick him.

He continued, "Not that we really are fooled by her stupidity anyway. I mean, they're, like, so fake. She just wants attention. She just wants out of badminton because she's an uncoordinated loser so she fakes some weird problem no one understands." "Christopher, if anyone is a fake I think that it's you and your stupid –" I began to say but was cut off by Ms. Gatzkin.

Seething, she said, "You two are ridiculous, you know that Blaire and Christopher? I should kick you out of my class, both of you. I just want to know what happened first. Should I call the doctor or something?" While adamantly speaking and shaking my head I replied, "No Ms. Gatzkin, definitely not! I don't usually get through more than a day or two without having an 'attack.' All the teachers are probably used to it by now." It was obvious that she was still very confused.

"Okay.... Well, since we got interrupted why doesn't everyone line up for a demonstration? I want to show you how to disable further plays by using a birdy smash move." I started to line up with everyone else but was abruptly stopped.

"Not you Blaire. You can just go sit on the mats for the rest of the period." "I'm fine, I don't want or need to-"

I was quieted by Christopher who mockingly said, "How do you like faking now?" I just wanted to die.

CHAPTER 7

Our grade 7 Phys. ED. Teacher was Mr. Fawcett. He was a no-nonsense, athletic middle-aged man (well, I thought he was middle-aged but he may have been younger). One particular day we were playing soccer which, at one time, I had loved. Now, though, scared of Phys. Ed and all sports because of the open-spaces they occurred in, I now hated participating in soccer.

That day, though, I played with gusto- until an unfortunate accident anyway. I started running with the ball, dribbling like a pro (or I would have liked to think so). I focused on the net several feet in front of me; I was certain I would score. Suddenly I rolled my left ankle. I instantly felt white hot, searing pain. I fell on the floor, clutching my ankle.

Bellanger was the closest to me and he stopped to help me. Acting tough, he told me to suck it up. Then he called Mr. Fawcett. They half-carried me to his office. A minute later, sitting in a gym office chair, I felt a lot better. Mr. Fawcett asked me if I would live (those were his exact words). Barely looking up at me from his paperwork, leaving me unsure if he even cared (though of course he did) he said, "Then I suppose you had better go to the hospital and have that checked out Blaire.

"Ms. Schmale" –the secretary- "will take you" he said. He wrote a bit more on his notepad before helping me hobble to the principal's office. I readily accepted Mrs. Schmale's offer to help me get my shoes on. She then led me to her car. We headed to the Edam hospital for x-rays.It didn't take long for the results to come back.

Michelle, the x-ray technician, said, "Well, there is a tiny line on the x-ray but I don't think it's broken, I think it's just a bad sprain. So ask one of the nurses for some crutches, and keep off your foot for a few weeks." Michelle smiled and we left. I thought about how fun I would have with crutches. They make you look cool -so that was my thought anyway. Crutches also happened to make me feel much calmer; I liked having something that felt like it enshrouded me. I couldn't wait.

***

The day after the gym incident, I sat watching TV alone up-stairs: Fabian and mom were downstairs and Nikki was outside with dad. I My stomach rumbled so I hobbled to the kitchen where I'd seen a muffin. I microwaved it for 12 seconds. While I waited, I heard what sounded like a vehicle moving outside and decided to take a peek.

I hobbled over to the window, not really scared at that moment. Still, my right side started shaking and my face went numb. I was having a hard time balancing. Before I had time to think, I jammed my left foot onto the floor to keep from falling over. Searing pain ran up my left leg and I slowly started to fall backwards.

From behind me I heard the microwave beep. It was ready; I was not.

CHAPTER 8

January 9th, 1995, is one day I will probably always remember because that was the day that (unintentionally) 'telling all' happened. Up to that point no one besides my immediate family –not even my close friends- knew about what I thought were seizures and this fear of open spaces/phobia-type of thing.

After eating my lunch one day I said that I was still hungry. I swear that in my entire high school career, I could have eaten just about non-stop. Some kid said that I should go to the canteen downstairs. I looked to Danielle to walk with me but I saw her no-where. Having someone beside me made my phobia of open spaces less horrid. Other fear-reducing tactics included hanging onto door handles and from lockers; lunging to a sitting position (sitting was not scary at all) when I felt panicked. Of course I made sure that the insane tactics (like the locker hanging) were never seen by anyone.

So since my best tactic was currently missing, to no one in particular I asked, "Does anyone, like, know where Danielle is? Did she take off to the bathroom and fall in a toilet or something cause, like, she's been gone for ten minutes." One of the boys in my class answered, "No you idiot, her mom picked her up for something-where were you Blaire?"

You've only got so long after saying you're going to do some-thing before you do it or else people call you on it. That was my current predicament- I'd said I was hungry and was offered a solution.My classmates expected me to go or explain why I wasn't. "Well," I began as I started painfully moving towards the door, "see you guys in a bit."

I tried not to panic but despite my self-helping, I froze. I felt the attack coming on about a nanosecond before it did. I had just a moment to lean against the door frame; I hoped it would keep me from falling over and save me some embarrassment.

My right leg started shaking and my right arm and my face went numb. My classmates looked on in confusion. Everyone watched the 15 second 'attack' and then looked at me as if to say, 'explain!' I wracked my brain hard for a reasonable excuse (ex: "I got a cramp in my leg, damn growing pains!").

Christopher's none-too-pleasant accusation broke into my thoughts: "Did you not hear me ask you during that 'thing'" –now I realized that they had not been waiting patiently for the 'attack' to be over but had been demanding an explanation- "what the heck you're doing?"

I blushed a very deep shade of red. Remi (not as cruelly as Christopher) said, "Yeah Blaire, like, what's the deal? I've seen you have those funky chicken things before on the bus and you tell me a different excuse all the time for why you have them, tell the truth."

I was stuck. I had to face the music and tell my classmates the embarrassing truth. Redundantly I said, "Well you guys, I guess I'll tell you. Know how I used to have seizures? Well, I think I still do."

What I didn't explain –because it didn't seem important- was that not only did I have seizures; I had some kind of fear of open spaces too. A fear that I figured was directly linked to the seizures. A fear that I thought came upon me when I was scared of being in an open space and then triggered a seizure.

Bellanger very cruelly rebuked my assessment of the seizures, "Oh come on Blaire, are you trying to be a doctor now?" I liked Bellanger but there were some times I wanted to sock him- this was one of those times.I seethed, "No Bellanger, I'm not, like, a doctor and I never said that I was.

"When I go in an open space I started having these attacks which I think are seizures like you just saw except they weren't so bad at first. Then after a while though, they got so that they're worse than now." I don't think my classmates followed. I wasn't too perturbed by this and I continued, "Anyway," I continued, "I can't help those 'attacks', and places like going in the gym are extra bad for me and stuff." I thought that I sounded logical and mature.

I was sure that everyone would just say –or at least think- 'oh, that makes sense, how astute of you Blaire to see that you have atypical seizures.' We would then continue to exist together in our classroom, they feeling a little bit sorry for me that I had to have these obviously un-fun seizures while being aware that I was not crazy.

Christopher ran his hands through the back of his hair. He condescendingly said, "So you really want us to believe that you can't help it that you're having these freaky things and all of this crap? Do you realize what your problem is Blaire and all of your talking and crocodile tears won't help you? You're just a diva."

I never particularly liked Christopher anyway but I was hurt. This was not at all going as I had thought. Confused, I said, "What are you even talking about Christopher?"

He retorted, "Oh come on Blaire," he began, "You are a drama freak and you think you're some hot shot actress and then you act crazy and all artistic and all of this crap. You're like a hippie from the 70s living in your own little flower world that doesn't make any sense and everyone thinks you're wacked.

"You think that acting weird and saying you have some medical condition or something is going to make people feel sorry for you or something? Get real." I was absolutely stunned. It took a few seconds to reply, "If anyone thinks they're a hot shot it's you

Christopher and I don't have the slightest clue why you'd, like, think that in the first place.

I shot defensively,"What have you ever done with your mediocre extracurricular talents and below average brain? Not to mention that your face kind of looks like a crater on the moon!"

"Blaire, just shut up," Nicolle snapped at me. I reared my head in her direction and said, "What did you say to me?" I thought I was getting a migraine even though I'd never had one before and didn't really know what they were like.

"I don't need your crap! And are you honestly trying to tell me you're agreeing with crater face?" -this was my nickname for Christopher that I'd never before said aloud.

Nicolle was generally my pretty good friend and I was shocked. She said in a placating but not too friendly voice, "Are you really that surprised Blaire? I mean, what you're saying is a little far out. Not that I'm sticking up for Christopher because I think he's lacking in genetic code that predisposed him to be overtly and surreptitiously discerning" -thankfully for Nicolle's sake I don't think Christopher understood.

"I thought you were my friend Nicolle and that of all the wacked out people in this class who worry about not much more than their little snobby groups, you would happen to understand me and realize I'm telling you the truth."

Roach cut in and said, "Snobby groups? Nice Blaire." Before I could defend myself to Roach he continued, "Christopher is right Blaire. You are a drama queen diva wannabe or whatever and you are making this up so you can just get the satisfaction of having the teachers feel sorry for you and pay attention to you."

I was very near tears. I really thought Roach was cool. Besides, he used to play soccer with me and I called him Roachie and he had said –if only for pretend- that he liked it. Being his friend had made me feel almost as cool as I had thought he was; that was all crushed in one second.

I took off for the canteen without a backwards glance. I ran away from all the kids glaring at me. Going around the corner I heard Jason (one of the nicest of the guys) saying, "Blaire, don't be so mad but seriously, what did you think we'd say when you told us...?" Then I was gone.

One hockey practice I got to talking to another hockey mom. Our conversation lulled, causing an awkward silence. I thought that we should be talking. I reasoned that otherwise we were all alone.

Then I had a second thought: I was not alone at all because the Holy Spirit was in my heart. I could pray to Him silently. I could just sit there and do nothing but watch hockey, but I was never alone.

I thought for a moment that it was probably the same thing for the other hockey mom; she was not really alone either. Then my second thought again came along. I don't think she had the comfort I did. I don't think she knew Jesus personally.

The thought made me very sad.

CHAPTER 9

While standing in the hall, after the first bell that signaled that recess was over, I heard the second, warning- bell, the one that says 'get to class now!'

The problem was that I also had another thing to do so I was faced with a 'dilemma': should I go to the bathroom -because obviously I couldn't have went during recess, I would have ended up missing a couple minutes of soccer- or should I go to class and have to hold it? I chose the former, obviously.

When I was done in there it was a couple of minutes into class. Miss Danielson opened the door before I could even get in the classroom and immediately told me to go to the principal's office.

It was only October 13th and I was already going to the principal's office. I mumbled all the way down the halls to myself about the injustices of school life.

On arriving I whined to the secretary, Mrs. Schmale, that the reason I was late was so I didn't pee my pants. Mrs. Schmale, a pale lady with freckles, glasses and short brown hair said, "No, it's not the principle you are to see. Your mom is here."

I looked around and saw that, just as Mrs. Schmale had said, mom was standing in the office. I thought to myself, 'seriously?! Miss Danielson hates me so much that she called my mom?!'

Mom walked toward me and put her arm around my shoulder.

I had no idea what was happening, "Okay Blaire, we have to go, see you later Mrs. Schmale."

I was weirded out and I didn't know what else to say. I lamely mumbled, "Wait mom, I have to pick up my book bag and my homework that Miss Danielson might have for me so I can get it done in time."

No sooner had the words left my mouth then I rolled my eyes at myself.

CHAPTER 10

I was actually not minding grade 5 as of September 25th -mom's birthday- 1992. It was grade four and I was nine and a half years old. My "previous, all-so-serious disease" was far from my mind. Any problem was far from my mind.

I was a tom-boy. I played soccer and stayed away from most girls most of the time. Getting hurt was an honor and crying was never an option. I wore scars and bruises like badges. I was sure my many friends adored me. The world was my oyster.

I was happy and carefree; my friends were great. We hung out at school playing soccer or playing "house." My family was awesome too. I had a lot of fun with my chubby little brother. I got quite a kick out of my harder-to-relate-to but adorable seven-year younger sister.

Our parents loved us so much. They taught me about my God; took us to church; and sent us to Bible camps, youth groups and all that sort of thing. They let us play every sport we wanted to. Dad let me stay up late sometimes when Alfred Hitchcock was on. We spent a lot of time together. Like how mom and dad took us on trips to the United States when we were younger and on a cruise when we were older.

My biggest problem was my school teacher, Miss Danielson. Well, I thought so at the time. She was my one and only teacher from grade four until the end of grade six. It seemed like she would never go away; just when I was done one grade and I thought we would get a new teacher who wouldn't take us on a class trip to Batoche for the –enth time, *she* was the teacher of my new grade.

I thought she was weird looking with her red hair and freckles. I figured she was the most humongous lady in the world (in hindsight I realize how exaggerated my imagination was) and disliked that too.The words she used (such as 'verbal diarrhea'), along with the sound of her voice, annoyed me. I cringed at almost everything that she did. She really was a great, kind, understanding teacher but I didn't recognize that. She just drove me nuts.

I talked back to Miss Danielson nearly every chance I got. She sent me to the hallway often. I said that I didn't care but it was a cover for something. I thought I needed to sound rough and tough but I kind of was not. By grade four I wanted to be like everyone else in school. I don't think 'nice little Christian kid' was the aura I wanted to give off, so I rebelled.

***

I found myself doing something I did at least five days a week, three times a day: playing soccer with grade four teammates such as Larry and Bellanger; Roachie, Remi and Aaron and the other girl, Chantelle. The grade five kids -who I thought were so cool- included my cousin Delbert; Jimmy and Randy. They were just the best.

I was on Roachie's team and we were playing Aaron's team. I had just finished yelling, "Hey Joey"- that was another cousin and a third grade teammate- "I'm open! Pass it to me!" That's when I heard that 'it' happened.

I called to Joey for the ball, but don't recall it getting to me. Then like a crazy warp in time the ball was sitting in Aaron's net; I stared at the net and everyone else stared at me.

I yelled, "You guys, the ball is in Aaron's net, isn't someone going to do something?" No one was making a move so I took step forward to do it myself. I saw my big cousin Delbert coming at me. He just put his hand on my shoulder, pushed me back and just said, "Blaire, explain."

Delbert and I were at my house: Delbert was five and had just started kindergarten but it was his day off. Kindergarten seemed a million years: I was only four.

While his and my mom visited inside, he and I sat on my 'thinking rock' beside the house. We were making mud pies with leaves on top. Admiring them Delbert said, "These look really cool, think we should eat it Blaire?" "Yeah, they look nummy but I don't think we should eat them cuz mom might get not happy if we do that."

Delbert hesitated but said, "I guess you're right Blaire. My mom probably wouldn't think it was great either. And besides, we might die if we eat dirt."

I looked at him, accepting his logic and said, "Yeah, we might choke and fall over. Except we are already sitting down." Delbert nodded at me and said, "Yeah, I don't want to choke, I don't think it's very much fun. I saw a show on TV where a guy was choking on something and then he died.

"I don't want to die because it's kind of scary." I looked quizzically at Delbert: "Why are you afeard of dying? Do you think that it'll hurt really lots and then you'll get creepy crawlies on you?"

"No, I don't know if it would hurt or not. Unless you got your head cut off or something, cuz that might hurt. I just don't know what happens when you die." That was when I recognized the chance to share the most important thing with him ever: "Do you want to be able to know for sure for sure that you are gonna go to heaven sometime...?"

CHAPTER 11

It was grade 4 math class and I was seated with my desk up against the desk of my friend, Roachie's - this was part of the new 'desk buddy' seating plan. I thought that Miss Danielson had put fire and gasoline together when she let us sit in the same vicinity. I also thought 'desk buddies' was a stupid idea- I still didn't point out what I was sure was a mistake lest she correct it.

Generally I recoiled from learning anything in Miss Danielson's class. I assumed that Roachie did too. Math, though, was admittedly kind of interesting and we listened with rare attention.

Miss Danielson told us about measurements and weights. She then drew some horrible weight scale picture on the blackboard. Then she gave us homework. I thought she had taught very little on the subject before giving us homework to do it ourselves at home.

But 'meh', I thought, 'oh well.'

*

"What," Roachie asked me in the hallway on the way to library for our next class, "was that all about?" Shooting him an annoyed look I asked, "What *are* you talking about?"He shot me a 'you're stupid' look and said, "What on earth were you doing in class?" "You were there Roachie! What do you mean?"

Before we could say more my red haired, freckled friend Bobbi joined us. She said, "Yeah Blaire bear, what was that all about?" "Are you both going loco?" that was a word I'd just learned. Then, "You two were there. We got our new seating plan. Then Miss Forehead Wrinkle" –one of my many, immature, groan-able nicknames for her- "said that we had to do math."

They directed what I assumed was supposed to be a conspiratorial, pitying look toward me. Roachie whispered, "Blaire, why did you call Miss D fat?" I looked at him like he was from another planet and said, "Oh come on you guys! You know that I didn't do that. I mean, she's a fatso and all that but I wouldn't have said that!"

Roachie and Bobbi looked confused, "What are you talking about Blaire? Don't you remember the conversation? You said she was, like, fat and asked if she had a bathroom scale. Then she looked constipated," -Bobbi was the only person my age that used that word. "'Kay, you two are both crazy," I said shortly.

I then hurried till I was away from them and near the library. On entering the carpeted library I saw Mrs. Olson, the awesome school librarian, and I waved to her. Before I sat down I saw Bobbi and Roachie walk in together. I heard Bobbi say, "...I really don't think she knows."

*

I usually loved library. *That* library period was the worst ever. I was sullen and quiet and actually a model student. I caught Miss Danielson looking at me once or twice to see if I was ok. As a matter of fact, everyone in library that day was being very weird around me. When Jenine bumped into me she said sorry with a voice as mortified as if she'd just killed my dog.

Danielle and Chantelle often looked in my direction, giggled and then averted their eyes. Jamie, the guy sitting across from me, had snuck gum into the library. Without speaking he pushed some at me and smiled oddly. I couldn't wait for library to be over.

Finally the bell rang for recess but I didn't run to get my outside clothes on to go play soccer. Instead I grabbed a kid in my grade –Remi- by the arm as he tried to walk out of the library door.

I demanded, "What the heck is going on Remi?" I felt that Remi would have to be honest with me. We went on the same bus so I felt we shared some sort of wacked out bond.

Pretending not to hear -or understand- he said, "Hmm?" and lifted his chin uncomfortably. "Oh come on Remi!" I accused, "Don't give me that b.s. man! Like, everyone is talking about some wacko thing that happened about me calling Miss Danielson fat or something, and I want to know what's going on!

"I never said that, and before you think I'm getting soft and mushy and stuff, get real! I don't give a frig' about making sure I don't hurt Miss Freckle-face's feelings. But at least if I said something mean I think I'd remember so I could take credit for it."

By the look on Remi's face I could see that he was seriously considering my twisted, cold rationale. He replied: "...we were just sitting there listening. Chantelle and Danielle" - (yes, 2 of my best friends' names ended in -elle) -"raised their hands a few times to say how the class was so interesting. I felt like saying, 'barf' and I turned around and realized you and Roachie were doing the same thing."

"Yeah yeah, I remember that part you idiot. Get on with the part I don't remember." "Okay, well anyway, then I saw you turnaround and listen to her really interestingly" -I interjected, because I may have thought school was dumb but I loved English- "Interestedly you mean?"

"Yeah, yeah, whatever, am I telling this story?" he said in a voice that was reserved for kids my age. He then took a breath and continued, "So Miss Danielson started talking about grams and milligrams and all this. And we listened to her talk about that for a few minutes. Then you got a really funny blank look on your face and said, 'Miss Danielson, do you have a scale at home? Do you weigh yourself? How much do you weigh?"

I grimaced but he continued as if he hadn't seen me, "'Kay Blaire, I know that you're pretty out there with all the stuff you say to her, but I don't think you should ask your teacher that." Then he walked away.

*

An issue that seems life or death for a kid one minute can be as if it never happened the next. That's what happened shortly after library regarding my episode of calling Miss D fat. It almost slipped into oblivion and if left alone, would never be remembered again. I went home on the bus that day.

I never told my mom about the days' events. I wasn't trying to lie by omission, I just forgot all about the days' events which seemed insignificant. I spent the next two days at school equally oblivious.

SCREAM

The Birds' song should make me happy
But instead I cry.
The Birds have no worries and
Sing Joyously.
The Cat's purr should make me smile,
But instead I sob,
His fur is so delicate
And soft to the touch.
The Turtles bathing on the rocks should make me laugh
But instead I only scream.
They are so silent and slow,
Persistent in their movements.
I cry when I hear the Birds
For my worries
Are incomprehensible
And harsh.
And I sob when I hear the cat's purr
For unlike his fur
My heart is as
Hard as stone.

I scream when I see the sunbathing Turtles
For when I am silent it is for the fear
Penn up inside me and when I am slow
It is because I can't go on.
I want to be happy when I hear joyous sounds,
I would like to smile when I see happiness,,
I would love to bathe in sunlight like I should.
Instead I only cry. Sob. And scream.
Of how it should be. But can't.

SECTION 3: BIG BOSS HEAD

Family is hard- they drive us crazy, while we are totally unaware that we are doing the same to them.

Now add to that a sickness that requires a lot of Mom's and Dad's attention. And involves a lot of dramatics and bellyaching and screaming and crying.

And siblings who just can't understand that there actually is something wrong because it sure doesn't look like it.

Fabian was caught between a rock and a hard place. Nikki was stuck with a sick, needy and overdramatic, 7 year older sister. Mom drove me to doctors and psychologist and dad, at home, tried his hardest to keep me as sane as possible by being immensely compassionate.

Resentment bubbled under the surface at almost all times. Who was resentful of whom was the question at hand.

****

CHAPTER 12

You know those siblings that are inseparable and rarely fight? Yeah, well that wasn't my sister Nikki and I. At all. I was 7 when she was born and partly due to it, we never really bonded... and I was awkward with her from day one.

Nikki never adored me; she never wanted to be like her big sister Blaire and I didn't feel overly loving towards her. When the 'attacks' began, one could even say that I resented her.

The peak of our fights and misunderstandings probably was when we were 14 and 7. I never thought she understood me and I was sure she would never try. I thought she had a perfect life with no worries. She was surrounded by friends -real friends- when I hardly had any.

She was fun and adaptable. The worst was thinking that dad loved her more than me. Nikki's life seemed to be fun moment followed by fun moment yet she seemed to dislike me. I wondered why she could possibly resent me so much. She couldn't have been jealous, so what was it?

I wondered if she disliked me because I never was happy enough to adore her. It perplexed me.

***

One November day in 1998, grade 10, I had a fit to my mom and dad but that was something I did often so it wasn't too surprising. It was also not surprising for me to scream about the injustices of my horrible, sad life. This time, though, I also said bad things about Nikki.

I screamed about how I was so desperate and dejected, alone and misunderstood and she was so... well, not: "She is such a little brat and she only cares about her perfect little self and making forts and getting dad to make her a samurai sword"- he had welded one for her one time- "and all that crap.

"I am stuck in this little shell of mine that I should be wanting to break out of but instead I have to just wish that it was even smaller so I might not be as terrified. Nikki hates me and I don't know if I like her much better either. She has no idea what true pain is." To dad I said, "And I wish she knew!"

Dad rarely got mad at me because he knew how much pain I was in. That time though, Dad did: "Did you just say that you are aware of how horrible your own situation is and you still actually wish that Nikki had to suffer the same way?"

I just nodded my head in turmoil, trying to suppress tears. I threw my hands up in the air, "Yes dad, I just did. She doesn't know my pain and doesn't care at all about me. I wish she knew what pain is."

He said, "I cannot fathom how horrible you feel Blaire and I try very hard to not upset your fragile, tormented world. But I will not abide you speaking like that about someone that you love and that loves you."

I retorted, "Well, sorry dad but that's how I feel and I'll be damned if I change it until she cares."

I often compare life to TV (weird, I know). One episode of CMT's 'Reba' is about a school fundraiser. For years Reba had successfully headed it until one particular year.

One year she had to do it with Barbara-Jean, the woman that stole Reba's husband. Reba directs B-J to do the fund-raiser like Reba had other years. Barbara-Jean ignores almost everything Reba says.

The fundraiser turns out wonderful so they threw an after party. Reba decides to embarrass B-J by telling everyone that she did not choose to do the fundraiser with Barbara-Jean. Barbara-Jean is an annoying know-it-all whom Reba doesn't want around.

But trying to formulate a good way to say mean things, Reba got her words twisted. She said complimentary things about her co-chair... but did Reba actually get her words twisted?

This was how I felt toward Nikki. I both said and thought mean things about Nikki. I tried to convince myself consciously that I believed what I said and heard in my head.

I felt hurt by her –in hindsight I realize she probably was hurt by me as well. The truth was that Nikki had and has an inescapable grasp on my heart.

I ran to my room and threw myself on my bedroom floor. I cried and I cried and I cried and sobbed. Finally the tears would hardly make their way down my cheeks anymore.

In my dresser was a notebook I used to write poems and thoughts in. I ripped open the dresser; pens, notebook and every-thing else falling out with a bang. I don't know how mom and dad managed to ignore these –and other similar noises- that often came from my room.

I decided that I hated Nikki. I hated my dad for being mad at me for being mad at her. His words had only confirmed my prior suspicions: he loved her more. I cried afresh in agonizing despair. I was mad at him but I was even madder at her.

I knew no way to hurt her like I thought she had hurt me but I wanted to. I decided to write hateful things about her. It might at least make me feel good.

INNOCENCE
The tears pour down my face,
Because I know the pain,
Being separated in time and space,
With nothing left to gain,
She is so small and unaware,
She doesn't see me cry,
She has not a single care,
And knows not that of I.
My fears surround me all the time,
Her laughter fills the air,
For her to understand reason, rhyme,
For her to learn to care.
But how can I stop her spirit from running free within the skies,
I could be so mean and cunning,
Crush her in my vise.
But her innocence I'll leave alone,
I won't crush her with my fears.
I'll leave her to wander and roam,
I'll hide her from my fear

I looked at the paper when I was done. Very few of the words that I thought I felt toward her were on the paper. What I wrote was kind of the opposite of what I thought I wanted. 'Where,' I thought, 'did those words come from?'

I will love Nikki -we may not always understand each other- but I will always and forever love her.

CHAPTER 13

It was a beautiful June Sunday in 1997 and church had just let out. Mom, dad and Nikki were talking to someone. When I saw Fabian heading outside I followed him as closely as I could; I just wanted out of there.

Once outside, I stood on the ramp in terror. After noticing me following him, Fabian ran to the parking lot to taunt me with what was a crazy easy task that I still could not do. Standing there in fear, I never noticed the softness of the breeze; I never really noticed the kids laughing; I did nothing but *feel anxious*.

Fabian seemed to relish hurting me and I was mad at him. Still, there was something else; I loathed myself and everything else too. I felt alone and abandoned; I wanted to abandon others too but I couldn't even leave the ramp for dread. Fabian knew every single one of my buttons to push. He resented me and maybe hated me too. He didn't like what it had done to his life.

So Fabian used what he knew so intimately –my phobia and my 'attacks'- against me and he relished doing so. I looked down at him from the ramp which Fabian knew I was too terrified to leave. "Get back up here!" I hissed. He was at least six feet from the ramp but I could clearly see the morbid enjoyment on his face.

"Now why would you want me to do such a thing?" Fabian asked in mock innocence. That was a type of speech that he reserved for moments like these. Fabian acted relatively, decently, normally 'brotherish' to me while our parents or really anyone else was around. They didn't know that he was such a horrid little scummy jerk to poor me.

"You know damn well why!" I hissed even louder and then looked around to make sure no one had heard me. "I want my book and you know where it is...! And because I'm scared, okay?" I said the last part in an even lower whisper.

"Your precious book is in the truck, right?" he asked innocently although he knew that it was. "Yes! They are taking so long in the church that I want my book to read!" "So... you want me to come up there and walk beside you to the truck so you can read your book?" Fabian asked.

Dumb, desperate me, I overlooked his sarcasm; I thought he wanted to help me. Now was the perfect time to make the dagger he was about to stab in my heart stick. "Well then," he said while backing away from the ramp another two steps, "just come down here." I took a couple steps to follow.

Suddenly I realized that I was a fool. I ran quickly back to my spot on the ramp, holding the rail. I looked like a terrified deer in the headlights, but I didn't have an attack. Fabian continued to taunt, "Oh, that's right, this is an *open space.*

"And you don't do open spaces because the great boss genius in your mind told you that open spaces are bad, bad, bad. Because if you come in an open space you might freak out and fall down and do the funky chicken and we know how bad that would be because then you wouldn't be *in control.*"

I should have been flattered that Fabian seemed to know me better than I knew myself... but I wasn't. I hated him - I hated him with every fibre of my being. And I loved him at the same time which made hating him hurt that much more. The opposite of love is indifference; love and hate are actually painfully similar.

I felt absolutely destitute, exposed and helpless. A tear slipped from my eye but I would be damned if I'd let Fabian see. Or anyone else for that matter.

I tightened my grip on the ramp railing and turned my head sideways, somewhat out of his view. I was such a nervous mess that just the small movement from facing the parking lot to facing the church nearly threw me into an 'attack.' Though I couldn't exactly see him with my head turned, I heard Fabian speak and knew his arsenal was not empty.

With faux sincerity he said, "I guess you'll just have to keep standing on that ramp and holding that little railing until mom or dad come out and help you." What could I say? He was right. I waited until dad came out of the church, he and Lyle laughing about something.

Finally dad noticed me, "Oh hello Blaire. I thought that you would be in the truck waiting for us and reading your book. To my brother he inquired, "And what are you doing standing here?" Fabian said oh-so-nicely, "Oh hi dad, are we going for Chinese?"

Dad took my arm and walked us to the truck.

CHAPTER 14

The last year of Fabian's elementary career came on September 4th, 1996. It was an exciting moment for him, though he never would have admitted it. He was excited to be the center of attention in our house for one day.

Mom took our pictures as we got on the bus. There was a routine when the bus came every first day. Mom (camera in hand) would walk with Fabian, Nikki and I to the bus doors. Nikki would have her picture taken and go to her seat.

Fabian was next but after his picture he would go up the bus stairs and stand by the first seat. After my picture was taken I would go up the stairs and Fabian and I would walk to the back of the bus together. Fabian and I never spoke the routine but we knew it well. I expected this would be the case forever.

After my picture was taken I glanced back to see Fabian but he was not there. A look through the window showed him to be in his seat. Odd this was, yes. Was I worried though? No. I was a little nervous when I had to seat myself without him, but I thought little of it.

When we got to school I expected Fabian to be stuck to me till we got to our respective doors. When the bus stopped, Fabian ran to the front; I had to walk the aisle alone. Now I was past nervous. Before stepping off the bus, I looked around, trying to be hopeful.

What I saw, though, made me anything but; Fabian was halfway to the elementary school doors with Shane.

I froze inwardly and I feebly squeaked out, "Fabian?" He turned and I was sure that he meant to come back to me. All he said, though, was, "Have a good day Blaire." Then he turned to Shane and they ran, laughing and smacking each other on the arms, to the doors.

Alone without Fabian I had no idea what to do so I panicked. As one might expect, so began that morning's first attack. As my leg shook I fell onto the ground on my butt, unable to speak, my face frozen. Twenty five seconds later I looked up. Remi stood beside me and Judy looked down on me from the driver seat. With her hand holding the door lever, she asked if I was alright.

She had seen me have several of these 'attacks' before so she wasn't too worried. I said I was fine and she nodded and shut the bus doors. Remi and I walked into the school together. He said, "That must be, like, the step of doom or something, hey?" and laughed. I was unamused and demanded,

"Why would you say that Remi?" "Well, like lots of times when you get to the bottom step on the bus you fall over and shake and your face gets stiff like a statue." I shot him a mean face. "Well sorry Blaire, I never meant to offend you but it is kind of like the step of doom." I put my palm up against his chest to stop him. Annoyed, I said, "No Remi, it's not."

I walked alone with feigned confidence through the double doors (it was really easy toact confident after Remi had walked with me most of the way and I'd just had an 'attack').

"God goes with you to fight for you against your enemies to give you the victory." Deuteronomy 20:4.

I saw that verse nearly every day on the door to the basement of our house. I've thought -without often being conscious of it- about that verse a lot over the years.

God is YOUR God. Not just some vague, distant God who happens to care about the world as a whole; He cares about YOU. And when He's allowing you to suffer –another way of looking at that, actually, is that He's refining you.

Isaiah 59:1 says, "Behold, the Lord's hand is not so short that it cannot save; nor is His ear so dull that it cannot hear."

He not only will fight for YOU, He always hears you (take this personally!). DO NOT FORGET THE PROMISES OF DEUTERONOMY 20:4 OR ISAIAH 59:1 (among many)!

Sometimes God will literally fight off enemies like cancer or MS or starvation. Sometimes He doesn't and sometimes it's not fun but He says He will be with us THROUGH the fire, not that there won't be fires.

He can help you fight by giving you the inner strength and peace to go through things. Fear and pressure might be there but you don't have to worry and fret.

CHAPTER 15

It was half way through the year of grade 7- so that would be 1996. I had always considered Fabian 'mine' in the way that he belonged to me, but now he was my protector too. Sure, he was only in grade four when 'it' began but he was very much a large part of my 'get to school safely' (or sort of sanely) routine.

I would have been intensely happy to never change. Fabian would walk right beside or in front of me (not behind, because I did not like being able to not see him and know whether he was near). When the bus would arrive at school Fabian would get ahead of me in the aisle. Together we would file off the bus.

Once off the bus he'd walk with me halfway to the double doors of the high school end. We'd wait until Remi caught up to me though I don't think he was ever aware of the role he played. After school, I would stand by the school doors, waiting for Fabian to leave the elementary end of the school and get me. We'd walk to the bus together, looking like merely loving, close siblings.

I loved our routine because it served me well, but to Fabian maybe it was not so much of a blessing. He still helped me without grumbling much though. I could always count on him. If asked, I would have said that it was our beehive of 1995 because in everything I had my brother Fabian. We were a funny couple:

I was a talkative kid who wore my heart on my sleeve. Fabian was a hush-hush kid who possibly never even had a heart (kidding...

maybe). I was little and full of energy. Fabian was pudgy and slow. We were Jack Sprat and his wife... sort of. He was my confidante in life and I loved him.

Our childhood was so much fun together. I dragged him around (even though he was almost as big as me) and involved him in all my schemes. When I hid in the closet with a sweatband on my head, he was there with one of his own (I didn't know what a sweatband was for but we lived in the '80s). Playing outside in the mud, he was there.

No matter what, he was there. When the 'attacks' started there was one constant- Fabian. At the end of a crappy day at school I would run to the bus to talk to him about it.

On the bus I sat near Remi but there were just some things I wanted to share with Fabian only. So when Judy –the bus driver- dropped Remi off I'd spill to Fabian. I'd turn to him, poke his often-sleeping, slumped pudgy figure and say, "Fabian!" "Fabian, wakey wakey!"

He'd mumble, "I'm tired Blaire, what do you want?" I'd say, "Oh Fabs, wake up and come here." Our cousin Shane usually sat next to Fabian. He usually tried to eavesdrop in but I'd quickly push his inching-ever-closer-to-us self away and say, "No Shane, not you! I have to talk to Fabian! Here," I moved over and patted my seat, "you can sit with me Fabian." He'd say, "Blaire, what makes you think I want to sit with you?" I'd just grab him by the arm and pull him over.

I always had some story to tell Fabian. It usually ended with something like, "... so see, it's been a terrible day. I swear I'd cry but we both know that's just not going to happen." Fabian usually took a few minutes to digest my story and then he'd say something like, "Oh."

I would whisper-yell, "Is that all you can say Fabian?! I have a horrible day and then you just"- but Fabian would cut me off and say, "I just meant 'oh, that sucks.'" "Yeah," I would say, "'sucks' would be the word. Do you have any idea how embarrassed I was? Except that I can't just go around and let people know that I was freaked out and embarrassed and stuff."

"Right," Fabian said in a way that was edging on sarcastic but I always let it go. I loved those times with Fabian.

HOLD ON

I am as vulnerable as a small child.
The tears pour down my young eyes
For as young as I am
I still feel unrecognizable pain.
I am so terrified,
The voices I feel inside
Are fireworks
When I'm scared of bright lights.
You say you understand
But you don't because you can't
But you still hold out your hand and
I take it because I need someone.
Don't leave me when your hurt so
Bad from watching me and
When my pain is almost your own,
Still don't because I'll wither away.
Even though you know that
Your pain would subside so much
If you only would let go,
Don't. Because as young as I am

I still know.

SECTION 4:CRADLE WILL FALL

I was almost what you'd call a 'regular.' Well, that's not totally true. I didn't spend weeks there like some people have to do. But it seemed that just when I thought that I was done with that place for good, I was back. 16, 13, 10, a baby.

Oncology... well, before I knew what the word meant, I had had many appointments there. Vials of blood, tubes in my head when they couldn't find a vein anymore.... I even still have two small scars on my right side from the tubes that were put in there.

Neurology... that was also a word that I learned at a young age. This made me feel mature in a weird way. That I knew that I mean. It's funny, the thing we sometimes think are interesting.

Oddly enough, most of my visits took place in pediatrics. They have different departments but only one Blaire....

CHAPTER 16

I had been at this whole seizure/attack and phobia thing for approximately 3 years now- I was in grade 10 and really in need of some drastic changes.

Dad rarely came to the Royal University hospital with us. That was one of the reasons that day was memorable- he stirred things up a little. I wasn't ready for it but surprise, surprise because I wasn't ready for a lot of things that happened to me on a daily basis. What is that saying, 'doing the wrong (or mean) thing for the right reasons?'

Dad was holding my arm. We were near the cafeteria in the main mall. The main mall of the RUH is a big hallway that branches off into smaller side hallways. The pediatric neurology department where Dr. Lory worked was down a small hallway.

That day, though, we weren't going straight to Dr. Lory's office but meeting him at the cafeteria. It's quite congested there. There are tables to sit down at and eat your food or visit, not to mention the long, winding lines of admitting very near-by. And always a lot of people, something that I kind of liked.

Unfortunately, the people didn't know that I needed them to stay close to me in case I became scared and/or had an attack. Having people all around me was only good if I was in control of every variable. So Mom and dad walked fairly close to me. An 'attack' was quite far from my mind. After a few minutes I spotted Dr. Lory in the distance.

When he saw us he nodded in our direction. He looked almost nice and I smiled at him and waved him over. Dr. Lory joined dad and I (mom was walking a few steps ahead by then). Dad shook his hand. In his South African accent he said 'Hillo Bleere.'My plan for us was to just grab a bite to eat and then head to his office.

*

The cafeteria tables were nearly within reach. I was getting closer by the second to having dad on one side of me and the tables on my other. I felt quite content and safe. Then all of a sudden, dad let go of my arm. He walked to a spot about six feet from me, leaving me standing alone and terrified.

It was like when you see a movie happening in slow motion through one of the characters' eyes. I heard two Hutterite ladies talking to each other. I saw a boy with no hair sitting with his parents and I thought that he probably was going through chemo. It seemed like a very slow dawning on me that I was relatively alone and left to fend for myself.

The noises in the hallway all seemed to halt at the same time. I felt my right toes tingling and had time to think, 'oh no, this is it. Hopefully I don't hit the floor too hard.' I even found time to glance at the brownish-orange checkered tiles below me and think they were pretty unstylish.Then I was down on the floor, my right side convulsing and my eyes poised at the ceiling.

After about five seconds, I saw dad coming towards me. Soon after that, I 'came out of it.' I pulled myself up, hanging onto dad's arm. I could no longer see Dr. Lory so I asked where he had gone. I looked around and saw him near the cafeteria cash register, holding a little notepad and writing something.

"So that was it then?" he asked as he finished writing in his note-book and walked toward us. Dad brushed off his knees which were dusty from the floor before saying, "Yes Dr. Lory, pretty much all of them are like that."

"I see, and so she falls over almost all of the time then?" I was irate at how they talked about me like I was a specimen... or a baby. Getting my voice back I demanded, "So what's your deal dad? You just left me there to take care of myself?"

Soothingly he said, "I understand your anger Blaire," dad began in a placating but none too guilty voice, "but I had to. I am sorry if that was unpleasant for you honey, but Dr. Lory had to see you have an attack. Leaving your side was the best way to bring one on."

It was a good thing it had been dad to momentarily breach my trust like that. Anyone else, I probably would have stayed mad much longer. I thought his reasons were good and rational as much as I hated to admit it to myself. I understood why he had done it. I thought, 'About time someone actually *does* something around here' but I thought it. I was a walking contradiction... or something.

During the attack mom had started ambling away from the cafeteria and toward us. I say ambling because she never hurried or seemed worried. Mom joined the conversation: "Blaire, it was a good thing. I know you aren't totally happy that we had to do that to you. Now Dr. Lory has now seen one of your attacks firsthand which is a lot better than him just hearing us describe them to him and trying to treat you that way."

I clasped my hands in front of my face and said, "Whoa whoa whoa mom. Are you saying that those EEGs that he subjects me to and that fun time we had walking down the hall with those morons were pointless. I mean, since 'Dr. Lory didn't see me have an attack first hand before but now all that's been solved?'" Mom put her head down, ran her fingers through her hair and sighed as if she was too tired to have this conversation right now.

She said, "Blaire, we both know that nothing has showed up on those EEGs. As for the video tape.... Well, I don't know what Dr.

Lory did with that video tape but anyhow, this was a good thing and I just wish you could see that." Trying to lighten the mood Dr. Lory just said, "They have good soup here," and he headed into the cafeteria.

Truth be told, I appreciated him for a moment.

When the Israelites –God's chosen people- left Egypt they headed excitedly for Canaan, the land that God had promised would be theirs. Almost right off the bat, though, they hit a road-block:

They found out, though, that the inhabitants were big and strong. God had promised to go with them and fight for them but he people, thought that God couldn't or wouldn't do *this*.

They said, 'nope, we can't go against these guys'. Since they ignored His promise, He made them wanderers in the desert between Egypt and Canaan for 40 years. They wandered until all the disbelieving Israelites were dead. The direct voyage from Egypt to Canaan was less than a month but they wandered for years upon years.

I might have been able to become 'attack' –or at least worry- free- in the same figurative time frame.' Instead I chose the '40 years.' I don't mean that He would necessarily take the problem away. But knowing God is not AGAINST you and that He wants the best for you changes things.

Life is more tolerable. The bad becomes a little different. If I would have just trusted that He had a good plan for *me*, I might have felt a peace that surpasses all understanding (Philippians 4:6). My joy in Him might have become a small catalyst to having joy in my life (Jeremiah 42:6).

Pick up your Bible even if you don't think it could possibly hold anything good for you. Pray that God reveals something to your heart, even if all you can do is groan and not say any words at all (Romans 8:26).

And you know above when I said He won't necessarily take your problem away? Yeah, He very possibly won't. But God also says that we will find Him when we seek Him with all of our heart (Jeremiah 29:13).

And He says that we have not because we ask not (James 4:2). Trusting Him to take care of you (however He wills to do that) is kind of like seeking and asking.

CHAPTER 17

I was feeling pretty good in the early part of grade 9. I was sure absolutely 'normal' was really close. I might never have known what was really wrong with me but I didn't care. Thinking like that was probably why I didn't mind seeing him that time. I wanted to rub my happiness -that was not of *Dr. Lory's* doing- in his face.

*

We parked a pretty good distance from the hospital yet I did not hold onto mom's arm (as I would normally). Instead I skipped ahead of her. When we got to Dr. Lory's room I practically floated to the exam table. I dangled my legs like someone might do if they were feeling that all was well with the world.

When he entered, Dr. Lory said hello to mom, shaking her hand in greeting before acknowledging me. Then, with his arms folded -I assumed that was what a big shot doctor did, he turned to me. A little sardonically he said, "My, Blaire, you seem to be very happy and looking well. May I ask what this is due to?"

I wanted to shout, 'Yeah and it definitely doesn't have anything to do with YOU!' Instead I said, "I feel great and I have for quite a while, like at least a few weeks. Maybe all the bad has come to an end." I had to restrain myself from adding, 'Didn't see that one coming, did you?' He just smiled very briefly -and very dishonestly I was sure- before saying,

"Well everything sounds great. So what is happening in your life

Blaire?" I thought, 'He would just have to be so arrogant as to not be happy that I am doing well since he is not responsible. I said, "I don't know what to, like, attribute anything to exactly and I don't really think it really matters what gets attributed to because I'm really pretty really happy.

"I have one seizure," I was very sure to get point across that I was still sure I had seizures, "a day, max and they're not bad. I don't seem to be anywhere near as scared during the day as I have been in the past. I'm enjoying life. I can't say my seizures are gone but I am pretty sure they'll be gone soon and that'll be that.

"I guess it is okay that you didn't listen to me or whatever and you didn't figure it out because it's looking like I'll be okay." "This will probably be a short visit then," he replied, still sounding very sarcastic, "I just need to ask you to sit straight on the exam table.

Smugly I said, "You do what you have to do doc." Doctor Lory said nothing.

CHAPTER 18

It was now February 15th, 1997; I was beckoned to the RUH to get the results of the wacked out observation session from hell. On arrival we were ushered into our usual room. Dr. Lory sat surrounded by the same interns that I had seen a few weeks ago.

Dr. You'll-Never-Remember-My-Name-Because-It's-Weird or Dr. You-Don't-Like-Neurologists-Too-Much, spoke first: "Blaire, my associate here on my left, I and Dr. Lory are all neurologists." Evenly I said, "That's really great for all three of you.

"But maybe you could tell me something I don't know and maybe care about and tell me what's wrong with me and give me, like, some pills!"

"Well, you see," he continued, not meeting my eyes, "since we are neurologists we know quite a lot about the brain. From your scans we do not see the brain activity typical of seizures and…."

"What are you talking about?" Before he could answer I said, "Never mind. Let me tell you something that I didn't, like, have to go to med school for a gazillion years to be able to figure out: I have seizures."

He was about to speak so I held up my hand, "No, listen to me. What I have, I realize, do not look like the seizures I had two years ago or whatever, but they are still just seizures. I don't know about brain activity or anything but that's what I have, so figure out how to fix them!"

84

I looked toward Dr. Lory. He looked annoyed as if he was thinking, 'I knew she was going to get like this.' He said, "Well Blaire, let me tell you something-" "No Dr. Lory, let me tell *you* something. I want, like, some medication that will treat what I have. You might have to dig around for them but if you're a big fancy doctor then you can, like, figure it out."

He pressed both eyes shut and held them there for a second. Finally composed he calmly said, "What you have is not neurological, we are not sure what you have." "If you don't know exactly what it is that I have then how do you know that it's not because of neurologics?" As soon as the word was out I knew that I sounded amateur and dumb.

But before I could contemplate too much, he began speaking again: "Doctors Fernandez, Alli and I all think that you have a mental disorder such as a phobia because you seem to-" "Seem to what? Be scared of open spaces? Are you really sure that's true? Because of course I'm scared of open spaces! My seizures are scary and I seem to have them more often there than anywhere else.

"Or maybe I seem scared because falling down on your back sucks and I don't like it and so I, like, want someone around. And by definition I'd have to say that being in an open space indicates that no one else is very close to you. If someone is beside me, they make the open space not as open. Not that you'd get that.

Continuing my rant I said shrilly, "And if no one is near me then I cannot hold on to them for support if, like, I have a seizure and can't really stand up. And then that's why an open space seems scary." I finished, quite sure I had made a good point. His only answer was to ask, "Do your 'seizures' hurt?" he asked. I did not understand where he was going at all with this. I shouted, "No, they don't hurt! I've told you that before! Maybe get Dora over there to write something down and you'd know!"

He said while getting up, "Be that as it may Blaire, we are quite certain you have a mental disorder that we cannot treat. You should go see a psychiatrist. We can recommend some in the city here or in North Bat-" At that I threw my arms up in the air and said, "I'm out of here."

I heard mom, who had been sitting quietly the whole time, speak up and say, "I'll go and get her." She followed me out the door and put her hand out to me. "Blaire, come here." I put my hands on my hips and turned and sighed, not moving. After a few seconds had passed, though, I very begrudgingly started walking to her. Most of my fear at that moment was trumped by my anger.

*

Back in Dr. Lory's room everyone acted like I never spazzed and left. Pointing to a piece of paper he had started to write on, Dr.Lory gave us referrals, to some psychologists and psychiatrists. Mom looked down at what he was writing as if she believed him and not me. I shook my head at mom while holding back hot tears. I spit out,

"So you're buying all their crap too? I mean, about me having something wrong with my head only?" "I don't know exactly what to think." Then, after a pause, she said, "But the doctors should know if you have seizures.

"They took brain scans and examined the results and did not find any of the brain activity typical of seizures so maybe they're right. And they gave me a prescription for some medication." I grabbed it out of her hand and read it, "Tegredol." Mom said, "Yes, Tegredol. Who knows, maybe with a little therapy and this Tegredol, your 'attacks' might end."

Unenthusiastically but less angrily I said, "Well, at least maybe if I'm a loony toon maybe that's easier to treat than some crazy looking odd seizures." We walked out of the room together.

A few years ago my family decided to vacation in Calgary. Unfortunately, the week we wanted to go happened to be Stampede week.

One Saturday I spent at least an hour on the phone trying to book accommodations. My kids started to complain that they were lonely and wanted to play. I was making them sad they said.I told them that I was on the phone as a favor to them.

Just then God spoke to my heart. He told me to go play with my kids.

He said to try again tomorrow and I would find a hotel. Part of me did not want to trust. After all, it could have just been my own wishful thinking. The reasonable thing would be to keep looking before *every* room was booked up.

But I didn't give in to the *reasonable* thing, I gave in to the *right* thing. Then I woke up with the plans to search again.

The first hotel I phoned had reasonably-rated rooms. Not the cheapest but just about. When we arrived, we saw that the room was also huge.

Not exactly life changing, but a great testimony that God cares even about the little things. When God tells you to trust, just trust. James 4:7 says: "Submit therefore, to God. Resist the devil and he will flee from you."

Or, as I say to my kids, "Let God be in control. Don't do things that make the devil happy and he will run away from you."

CHAPTER 19

I said that the day that I unintentionally told all was maybe the most memorable of days in the first half of my teens. But I was wrong- January 24th, 1996 was *as memorable* if not more so.

Mom and I entered Dr. Lory's little exam room, Doris weighed and measured me and then we sat there waiting for Dr. Lory's arrival. He rarely kept us waiting long (at least he was punctual).

The RUH is a teaching hospital and Dr. Lory often had interns with him. So I thought nothing of it when I saw a new doctor come into the room that day.

I thought he was an intern and Dr. Lory would follow. I was wrong. Then a few more neurology interns and residents entered. For the most part, I disliked and distrusted Dr. Lory. Still, I was slightly unnerved that he was not at my appointment.

I mentally gave names to some of the doctors who entered. Two of them became Dr. You'll-Never-Remember-My-Name-Because-It's-Weird and Dr. You-Don't-Like-Neurologists-Too-Much.

Dr. You'll-Never-Remember-My-Name-Because-It's-Weird cleared his throat awkwardly and said with no preamble, "Dr. Lory's daughter is getting married in British Columbia. He and his wife are gone for a week. My colleagues and I plan today to do an electro-encephalogram –an EEG- on you. We want to monitor your brain activity; if it is abnormal and suggests seizures, we will know."

I thought, 'finally.'

*

In a Royal University hospital basement room (I wondered why the basement?) I changed into a hospital gown. The EEG *electro-encephologram electrodes were then stuck into my hair. Once I had changed The light-weight EEG monitor was strapped to an IV pole tethered to me. I had been transformed into a gaping-dress, antenna monster.

The doctors waited in the hallway. The first was short and very skinny –the camera looked like it weighed almost as much as him. He looked pretty stunned and unmemorable, with his boring mousy-brown hair and glasses on dull brown eyes. His balding head with hair sticking up completed the geeky owl look. It wasn't hard to come up with the name 'Hoot' for him.

The most notable thing about the first doctor was that he was holding a video camera in his geeky hands. Nervously and with quite a whine, I demanded mom tell me what the heck that guy had a camera for.

Her only answer was, "it will be good honey," and she let go of my arm that she had till that point been holding on to. I felt myself tense in fear and anxiety. Mom cooed, "Sweetie," mom began saying to me, "they want to take some pictures to review."

I opened my mouth halfway and shook my head back and forth slowly, scoffing at her. A seething requisition slipped out of my mouth: "What the heck are they taking pictures of for, like, reviewing?" Before anyone answered I threw my arms up in anger.

"Oh frig, never mind! What kind of circus do you have planned for me today? You would think that I"- I stopped midsentence. Mom was getting further away from me. The nearest 'lifeline' was the IV pole with the EEG machine on it so I grabbed it desperately.

To my chagrin, the pole was flimsy and slipped out of my grasp- it was not much of a consolation. All in a rush tears started pouring down my face. I screamed, "What the heck are you doing mom?"

My yell was full of anger and contempt but at the same time it begged her to come back to me.

Some doctor that I had not noticed till that moment stepped forward. "Blaire, now I understand how horrible you feel in this situation but if you would cooperate with us we would so very appreciate it." He folded his geeky little hands.

I felt like pulverizing him. Until I noticed the monumental five steps between us. I screamed, "Did you just say that you understand?" Then incredulously I half yelled, hall accused, "You understand?" He suddenly looked very uncomfortable.

He shifted his gaze from one doctor to the next and landed on the camera man. The lens was aimed at my angry, poorly-clad self. I onerously yelled, "And why are we in the basement?" which caught everyone off guard a little. They had not anticipated that question in that moment.

"Like, did you stick me down here in case I freaked out and someone heard? Was it because you are a bunch of yellow bellied cowards who like picking on little girls? Well, you know"- the doctor started saying but I cut him off. With anger and tears I shouted, "Why the he&# do you think that I need to be in this hallway in the first place? Don't you have somewhere better or something?"

"Here's the thing," one of the dull doctors said in a placating voice that didn't hide his condescension, "The usual EEGs of your brain are taken when you are lying on a bed in a small dark room. These generally show no brain waves suggestive of abnormal neurological activity. For this reason we thought that we should monitor your brain activity in a place you find threatening, like an open hallway."

Everything I had ever said to the doctors was practically being spoon fed back to me verbatim. Many times previously I'd said that my seizures were related to my fear of open spaces and vice versa. The doctors had never addressed any validity in what I said. Yet, under their own twisted auspices, they were doing just what

I had suggested but had been dismissed. I was filled with loathing and rage.

I quickly looked around me. I became overly aware of the emptiness of the space that I was standing in. There was nothing in the hall that I could grab onto except for the walls. Most hospital hallways have rails but not here. I felt terribly alone and horrified.

My anger dissolved a bit as fear engulfed me. From just behind me, mom saw me tense and knew I was very anxious. Trying to be reassuring and calming she said, "Blaire, it is okay honey." I thought that it could never be okay and I freaked out.

Still cooing ever-so-softly, mom said, "Don't scream honey, it will be alright." She came to my side and smoothed my hair. I hated the feeling of condescension that the gesture engendered. I was probably imagining things, but anything that resembles insincerity to a sick, scared, vulnerable person is terrible.

She said, "Lying down in a room with the EEG was not helping the doctors get the information they needed but if you are an open space your brain might show us something." Then Mom was again backing away from me. At least four feet after only a second. I so wanted her close to me though I was still seething at her. The desire to feel safe over-rides almost every single thought- ever.

I screamed to them all, "I don't care what the reasons are! This is horrible! You are all horrible! You have no hearts, I am terrified and you are as good as murdering me! What if I fall, who will help me? Are you just going to let me, like, fall on the floor?! These hallways are cold and scary, I will get hurt! I wish dad was here, I want dad!"

I continued to wail and wail but to no avail. I became more and more distraught and scared.... And even then, no 'seizure' came.

CHAPTER 20

A couple of weeks later I was almost over pouting. I really thought that mom had not listened to my concerns and though I was mad at first, now I was just disappointed in her. I found out I was wrong a week later when she took me to the Pediatrics wing –that I had went to as a baby and now for pediatric neurology- at the Royal University Hospital.

My usual pediatric neurology nurse, Doris, weighed and measured me. She then sent mom and me into Dr. Lory's familiar office to wait. When Dr. Lory arrived we made pleasantries and then he examined my reflexes. He made me follow his finger with my eyes and I contemplated that those tests were stupid- I know the reason for them now but then it seemed foolish.

I then explained to Dr. Lory what was happening, including giving my diagnosis of possible seizures. He replied, "Well this is a mystery, I am not sure. We will have to do some tests." I was not thrilled because I thought I had just offered him a pretty good idea and he had barely acknowledged it.

I repeated my question to him: "Dr. Lory, is it possible that these are seizures cause it really seems like it." "How do these seem like seizures Blaire?" Dr. Lory asked quite condescendingly. He gave no hint that he was going to ever consider my answer though. I was just some not-even-teenage girl while he was a big fancy neurologist.

"Well, okay, like for starters I feel weird after these things."
"Okay…," he said, as if he really found my explanation lacking.

Dr. Lory sat down on the corner of his examination table. He crossed his arms over his knees in anything but an open, listening pose.

I was a little off-put by his obvious skepticism. Despite this, I went on: "Well, I've thought lots about what these things could be instead of"- He interrupted and said "-instead of seizures?" "Yeah, instead of seizures. Like, I was thinking what else this could be.

"Seizures aren't super common so it's not a far reach to say that they're related to what I had. Yeah, they look a little different; the seizures I had a few years ago were absence seizures"- score for me for remembering the word- "but they've got to be seizures, right?

"And especially since you took me off my medication for absence episode seizures or whatever they're called, like, a year ago because you thought I'd outgrown my seizures. Maybe I just never and they're just back."

Dr. Lory patted me on the hand condescendingly. In a syrupy voice that I did not like at all he said with finality, "Well you don't worry about it Blaire.

"You just leave the diagnoses to the doctors and you worry about teenage things like"- he paused to think of something and finally said, "sleeping in on the weekends. It is unlikely that these are seizures because, from how you and your mother described them, they do not sound like the seizures you had when you were younger."

I wanted to strangle him for being so obtuse. At twelve and a half I was nowhere near being a doctor. Still, I was quite sure that seizures –even in one person- could present themselves in different ways.

Dr. Lory properly diagnosed me in no time before, what was stopping him now?

CHAPTER 21

It was not the day that changed my life exactly, but November 13th, '95 was a pretty big day. It was after school and on that particular day, I was in the kitchen with mom as she made cookies.

I had recently become "Clown" -a main role in a play called "Good-Bye to the Clown". I was gushing to mom about the awesome role, the awesome drama group, the upcoming festival and on and on.

While talking I shoved a cupcake into my mouth, finishing it in only about 2 bites. As I headed around the table to throw the rapper in the garbage, it happened: I walked into the leg of the table. It was just a bump but I suddenly paused mid-sentence.

"What happened Blaire?" mom inquired nonchalantly. I looked at my leg and rubbed my ankle. For some reason I didn't want to tell her, so I lied, "Oh, I just stubbed my toe, that's all." Mom just said, "Oh, okay. Well, be more careful." She turned back to the dough on the cupboard. I stood there for another few seconds, thinking.

***

A week later I randomly voiced some concerns to mom: "Hey" –I said awkwardly - "I'm sure it's not a big deal, but I think something is happening."

Mom was washing the kitchen baseboards. Mom, immersed in her work, replied without looking up, "Well if you're hungry there's some yogurt in the fridge and I think there's a box of Goldfish Crackers under the counter by the stove."

I said again, "No mom, there's seriously something weird happening." Mom looked up from the baseboard and said, "What's the matter now Blaire?" I said, "Okay, well, it's weird. See, one day I was by the table and I, like, stubbed my toe and then my leg started tingling."

Mom cut me off. In what she thought was a reassuring voice she said, "Oh, you probably just hit a nerve, it's nothing." She began to turn back to the baseboards.

I said a little more persistently, "No mom, that's not it. I was playing floor hockey after and I hit my leg and it never really hurt but my toe tingled again and even my arm shook a little and a teacher said that I looked far away when it happened."

Mom looked more serious: "Oh." I continued, "This happened at drama too and I just told Mrs. Young and Mrs. Sideroff and them that I'd stubbed my toe. "From the looks on their, like, faces I think they thought there was a little more to it than that. "And then it happened a bunch of other times too. And it's getting worse mom."

Mom cut me off and asked, "Which leg?" I answered, "Well, I doubt it really matters but it's my right leg." "Well that sounds like something," Mom said. "I know," I replied, "I bet you I'm getting seizures again. I mean, it would make perfect sense.

"I had those episode absence seizures or whatever a few years ago and then the doctors took me off my meds because they thought I outgrew them but I bet the doctors were wrong."

"Blaire, doctors usually know what they're talking about." "Mom, the doctors aren't God and they don't know everything." "Well speaking of God," she said, "have you prayed about it?" I rolled my eyes and said, "Seriously mom? Frick', this is something the doctors can take care of.

"Anyway, God knows my problems so He can fix them if He wants. I don't always need to pray about things."

CHAPTER 22

It was less than a month before summer holidays- only grade 6 to go through and then in September 1995 I'd be in grade 7- when someone at pediatrics neurology called us in.

On arrival Dr. Lory checked my balance by making me walk one foot in front of the other in a straight, DUI-ish line. Then he said, "I suppose you wonder why I called you here today?" Mom said, "Yes, we were not entirely sure but probably just another checkup I suppose because it has been quite a few months."

Looking at me he said, "Since we first saw you and I correctly diagnosed and began treating you over two years ago, Blaire, we have seen no seizures or any abnormal brain activity. We see no reason to continue with your medication. Even when we moved around your dosage to add the Dilantin placebo for the experimental drug study you were part of, you have remained steady.

"We are quite sure that your seizures were only childhood maladies. We think that you would be fine without medication. How does that sound to you Blaire?"

"Are you sure that"- but mom cut me off to finish my sentence. "-that her seizures are fully gone and she will be able to lead a normal life?" I wanted to say, 'mom, I have lived a normal life pretty much *all* of my life so what are you talking about?'

Trying to be encouraging he said, "My colleagues and I are very skilled and knowledgeable in our field. "We are basically 100% sure that she has outgrown seizures."

It was music to my ears... at the time.

CHAPTER 23

So there she was, driving me out of Edam. It was just me and her. I asked what we were doing. She didn't answer. She turned south and kept driving out of Edam... to somewhere.

I said statically, "Mom, where are we going? What's the matter?!" I was beginning to feel my control over that situation slip away (not sure what made me feel in control of it in the first place).

Mom put both hands on the steering wheel. She seemed nervous. She looked straight ahead and leaned back in her seat a little. Finally she said, "Saskatoon. We are going to Saskatoon Blaire."

With a confused look on my face I inquired, "Why are we going to Saskatoon mom? We don't ever go to Saskatoon unless we are going to the cancer clinic for a check-up- wait, are we going to the hospital cancer clinic? Because we were just there...."

"No, not the cancer clinic... but the hospital, yes." I began to understand and I did not like the implications. Grimacing, I put my hand on the door handle.

In a much higher voice than I meant, I said, "Just take me back to the school and I'll go learn some stuff in Miss Danielson's class, okay?"

Mom said in a pained voice, "Blaire, I can't do that. We need to find out what's going on." With desperation I said, "I can't even remember any of those things so I really doubt that they're of any significance." I thought that if I sounded intellectual mom would take me more seriously, "So I think that I should just go to school."

"Blaire, something needs to be done. You've had three of these episodes"- I cut her off. "No mom, I was only told twice by people that I kind of did something funny." Mom shook her head, "You had one standing in the hall this morning. Danielle told Miss Danielson who told me, so I phoned Saskatoon."

I was angry by that point and yelled, "Why don't you just mind your own business Mom?!" Not really realizing that my business was her business. "Blaire, I know you're mad but that is no way to speak to me. You are sick and we need to find out what is wrong and remedy it."

When a person is a shaken as it is, being called 'sick' or 'ill' is extremely maddening and condescending. I said, in a voice just below yelling, "Mom, there is nothing wrong with me!" Mom drove onward.

*

We got to Saskatoon's RUH just before 4:00 on Tuesday. We saw a nurse named Lillian –like my grandma McCaffrey. She told me that I was not going to get any tests that day. Mom and I unpacked our few hospital things and went shopping. The tests started the next day.

I learned the word 'neurology.' Neurologists, I found out, study the brain and how it functions. They try to diagnose and treat it when it is not working the way it should.

From what they could see almost immediately, I had petit mal (absence) seizures which were not too rare in children my age. I was given medication, the seizures stopped and mom and I were sent home. After only two nights and three days there. **I even had time to think about inviting Stephanie for a sleep over before I even got home.**

CHAPTER 24

They weren't sure if they should go along. I had been healed, hadn't I? They had taken ½ the liver -they had been told it would grow back, though, since I was only 8 months old.

But they were young, about 26, and they were intimidated. They thought, 'Big, experienced surgeons usually know what they're talking about. Maybe we should listen.'

So despite their misgivings, they agreed. They agreed to giving me something that was supposed to help me but might harm too. I was so small and it was 1983 after all.

CHAPTER 25

It was 4:00 p.m. in December 1983. I was 8 months old and mom was working; back then maternity leave only covered the first 3 months of a baby's life.

Grandma McCaffrey baby sat me while mom worked at the hospital. One day, after work, mom went to gramma's and on opening the door, heard her baby wailing.

She trotted up the stairs and asked, "Mom, where are you two and what is all that screaming about?" "In 'ere," spoken in a broken French accent. Mom opened the bathroom door.

Grandma addressed mom's first question by saying, in a sarcastic and tired voice, "What is the screaming about you ask? What screaming, I don't 'ear any screaming."

Mom picked me up and wrapped her in a nearby towel. She could now see grandma's exhausted face. She sympathetically said, "Oh mom, from the look of it you two didn't have such a grand day together, eh?"

"Whad'ever would make you tink dat Elaine? Would it be dat dis child never does anything but scream? I fed 'er Pablum and she screamed.

"I rocked 'er and she screamed; in grampa's lap she screamed. I tried to get 'er to have a nap and she just screamed. Nothing made 'er stop screaming."

"Is her stomach bothering her again?" mom asked, grimacing.

Grandma threw her head back, drained of energy. "Well Elaine, you should be a doctor if you figured dat out." They both laughed a little.

"Yes, 'er stomach has been bo'dering 'er today. She would eat nothing else, I tried feeding 'er but she did not even want her jar of Tutti Fruiti. She didn't even want it.

I tried everything else I could tink of. I rocked 'er, I sang to 'er and"- "Well, in her defense mom, that in itself could have made her scream." "'ilarious."

*

Mom just senses something was very wrong so when we left grandma's we went straight to Doctor Smith's house. Mom presented him her screaming child. Almost immediately the doctor saw that something was just 'off.'

After a short examination of my intensely grouchy self with the distended stomach, he turned to mom and with a serious look on his face said,

"Your baby has cancer. Go to Saskatoon tonight. Tomorrow could be too late."

*

Mom rushed home and told dad the prognosis. In no time all three of us were on the road to Saskatoon. At the Royal University Hospital, mom and dad immediately consulted with the doctors.

They said that I had a malignant tumor on my liver. "Tumors," the doctors said, "generally take one of two forms. The more common is often inoperable. It resembles fingers spreading from one organ to others."

The operable, more rare is basically a ball of cancer. The doctors did not expect to find the second type.

*

My parents called their families to tell them the news. No doubt they asked for one of the biggest prayers of their entire lives.

That night mom -as she has almost every time that I have been admitted to the hospital- stayed with me. Dad stayed with his brother, my Uncle Barney who lived Saskatchewan in Saskatoon.

Mom was a born again Christian: she prayed. My dad was still on the fence regarding this 'crazy new faith'. So when he got to Barney's he didn't pray, but replayed the doctors' conversation:

'This is not a time to mince words. The chances of her living are next to nil. There's only a five percent chance of making it alive off the operating table and then only a fifty percent chance of living through intensive care. Her cancer will likely resemble a hand with fingers outstretched. The 'fingers' will most likely be spreading out from her liver, infecting her everywhere. We do not expect the cancer to be contained.'

Dad tried to sleep. When he finally did, he dreamt 'The dream.' I was on the operating table. The doctors cut my abdomen open; the cancer was all encased perfectly on my liver in a glass ball.

One of the doctors picked up the ball of cancer and accidentally dropped it on the floor. The glass and the cancer that it entombed fractured into a million pieces.

***

Traffic was not so bad that morning; Dad got to the hospital shortly. Shorter yet, though, were the moments we had together before surgery.

Not many words were said before the doctors took me away. Not many words are needed in those moments. Mom's new Christian walk hadn't been a long one. At that moment she sent out millions of desperate pleas to our Father.

They were pleas to save her daughter. More than that, that His will be done. Secretly, a work was taking place in dad's heart too.

*

Four hours later Dr. McSheffrey and nurse Anne re-entered the waiting room. His face was not completely ashen and dismal and he did not say "I am so terribly sorry."

What he did tell them was that I was not out of the woods yet. He told them, "Be cautiously optimistic." I still had only a fifty percent chance of living over the next few days.

He also said, "When we opened her up we found something we weren't expecting. The cancer was all encased in a lumpy ball."

I like things to be clean-cut and precise. I like making plans and following through with them-well, the follow-through has become a little less important and rigid in my mind the past few years.

I am trying to let go of rigidity somewhat and think I often succeed. I just kind of like the ability to remind myself with a plan or a list of what I need to do and then try to follow it and accomplish goals.

When I first wrote this book, I titled one chapter "The Beginning of the End." Another was something like, "The End of the Beginning" and others included the words 'beginning' or 'end' in them.

Why did I do that? I like things to have beginnings and ends. I like things to wrap up nicely and make sense –if their apparent reason is not to be found while they're happening, at least at the end.

But there is often much more flow to life than we would

like. Sometimes 'flow' doesn't seem like the right word at all when our lives are full of tsunamis, typhoons and hurricanes.

When I thought the time had come that I could say that my beginning had ended, I felt full of pride. Of course I never admitted this to myself.I thought that my hurricanes and typhoons were over and I was proud of that fact in a "I know it wasn't me but it kind of was" way.

If you are like me –and though I'm not checking stats on that, I'm pretty sure the majority of people are- then the majority of you prefer things like I prefer them. You want beginnings and ends even if you don't express it that way.

You want smooth flowing waters, not huge waves and winds meant to capsize.

REFLECTION

I look at you,
And I
Wish that you could share
My world, just for a
Moment, and I
Could be part of yours
You can't understand
The way I feel
And I wish I could
Feel the way you do,
Feel safe, and sane, even
For a short while.
But life isn't
Glorious enough
To give gifts such
As these. Even for a day,
Even for an hour
And I must just reflect.

SECTION 5: MOIST CREVASSES

Somehow I kept it from them. I reasoned that they didn't need to know, I hid it and didn't tell them because I loved them. Well, what they didn't know might not have hurt them, but it hurt me.

The truth was that I was so full of pride that I didn't want to tell anyone more than necessary. Not even my family. I didn't want to be the different one. I didn't want to look weak, even to them.

****

CHAPTER 26

I used to think I could only have one seizure per day; that had changed. I had 'attacks' many times per day and almost anywhere.

One day, about 2 weeks into the grade 8, I had an extra-horrible attack at school. Devin, Jason, Ashley and Chantelle saw it all- I was so embarrassed. The right side of my body shook, I fell on the floor and my face went numb for at least thirty seconds.

That was bad enough but after school, I had to figure out a way to walk to grandma LaClare's without dying (or so I dramatically said to myself). Though I had no idea if my plans would work, I tried to make a battle plan for my day's after school excursion.

I would first need to get some friends to walk with me right to the edge of grandma's lawn; there was a big tree there. Of course, these friends could never know that they were my life-line. I had to try to trust that they would help me without knowing they were helping.

Four feet from that was a recessed stone pathway. They made the space appear a little smaller and less threatening. This would take me right to the steps which, though, had the opposite effect. They were hard cement, not at all my favorite.

Their narrow-ness, though, somewhat vetoed this. Narrowness made them appear small. I liked anything to appear smaller than it was. Obviously. I just had to follow approximately 6 steps up before reaching the top one, very near to the door.

I then would have another possible life-line: the door. I had many thoughts about door handles, cement versus soft floors and many other aspects of things' characteristics, and doors were no different.

Grandma's huge wooden door had all sorts of carvings and inlay in it; I loved it. If need-be, I could grasp onto the 1 centimeter deep inlay and hold on (that was seriously my thought).

After the door, I would walk into the house. Grandma's rocking chair was right there where she almost always was situated at that time of day. I would quickly step so that I was behind her rocker.

I would most often play with her hair which she just thought of as me showing my love. I did love her immensely so this action seemed not at all out of the ordinary but I had ulterior motives too.

It saddened me to use someone I loved like that, despite how important the reason was and though it was hurting no one. Still, I appreciated that this display gave me time to work up with the nerve to race from the chair to the couch to watch Wheel of Fortune and Jeopardy.

I was usually okay on the couch till our shows were over. Then it was time to walk very near grandma to the kitchen. All the while enjoying the soft, high-pile carpet... for obvious reasons.

The Bible says that if we are weary and heavy laden –which I very much was- we should give our burden to Jesus (Matthew 11:28). I didn't know- or at least *remember*- this until after I was a teen.

Just describing some–because there were many more- strategies made me tired. And I had 'tactics' and 'plans' for nearly every single situation imaginable.

For a few years before I entered high school, I started shying away from Him. I was scared that one of my school friends would ridicule me for devotion to some guy they could not see. I was scared my friends would leave me.

Then once the 'seizures' or 'attacks' -or whatever they were- started in high school I thought that God did not care about me at all; I had another reason to ignore Jesus.

I scarcely read my Bible or prayed and I didn't like church. No one –as far as I remember- ever told me that Jesus wants us to have abundant (John 10:10) and not just mediocre lives; meaning He wants us to rely on Him to give us peace and safety.

I don't remember anyone telling me that troubles didn't mean He had broken that promise.

I may have taken solace in Him if I paid attention to Him. Like I said a few chapters ago, I don't mean that He always takes away the problem.

When you really trust God and when you get YOUR plan to line up with HIS, then even having cancer or a horrible phobia feels purposeful and not as bad.

I may have realized that He asked me to love others enough to ask them for help and trust that they would give it. I know there's not a Bible verse that says that, but seriously, God wants us to depend on each other.

One thing that *is* Biblical is that, if one is close to you (ie: you tell them the truth about what is happening to you), they will help pick you up when you fall.

I'm sure grandma would have loved to help me any way possible if I wouldn't have just depended on tactics of my own making.

So I had made it into Grandma's house 'unscathed.' Also, albeit with terror, I had also made it to the kitchen table where we played cards. I had even walked down the hallway once to go to the bathroom.

I thought I was okay till Dad walked in the door and motioned for me to get ready. When I stood up, the blood started rushing to my head and my heart started palpitating.

All I could see were open spaces between things and not really the things themselves: spaces between one chair and the next; the distance to the wall that no one else noticed.

Tears welled up in my brown eyes which, obviously, caught him a bit- and grandma a lot- off guard. He asked me what was wrong and though I rarely surprised him, I *did* when I yelled in torment that I could not leave.

Grandma knew little about my phobia or my 'attacks' so she was extra stunned. She said, "It's okay that you have to leave Blaire, we'll finish visiting another day. Besides, you had better go home and let me recuperate from having my pants beat off me in Rummy this evening." It was sweet how she thought a grade 9 kid would cry at that.

I said, "Oh Grannycakes, I can't get up!" "What do you mean you *can't?*" Grandma asked with a forlorn expression. I looked from one to the other and then shouted desperately, "I'm too scared, that's why!"

Grandma put her hands over her mouth and blinked rapidly. I never understood what she was doing. She pleaded, "Oh Blaire, oh my Blaire, is it that horrible?"I didn't answer but to avert my eyes so she wouldn't see me cry.

As I did, though, I saw tears in Grandma's eyes too. I had never seen her cry before. She said, "I would do anything to be able to take your pain away and put it on myself. You're so young, why does this have to be?"

Dad took off his boots and came and grabbed me up in a bear hug. Gently he coaxed, "Blairesy, get up, it's okay." He helped lift me out of my chair and walked me to the boot mat (which was only a couple of feet away but I could not walk there alone).

Dad said, "Go grab her shoes please will you mom." She ran, with her hands still over her mouth, to the living room door and then ran back to us.

Dad helped me put my shoes on. He was careful the whole time to hold onto my arm so I didn't freak out more. Then he motioned grandma to come and hold my arm so that he could get his boots on as well. Everything that he did was meticulous and well thought out. I needed meticulous and well thought out and it resulted in my adoration of him (among other reasons).

Dad put his arm around my shoulders and we walked out the door. Grandma stood in the doorway saying, "Oh I will pray for you Blaire!"

CHAPTER 27

For most of grade nine I had been sure of my imminent re-covery-I wasn't sure how that was going to happen but it knew it *would*. That's why when I started declining yet again later in grade nine, I was more depressed than ever before.

***

The church I attended was the Edam Pentecostal Full Gospel Assembly. One Sunday I went to church but I did not attend- I was just too scared to enter the building so I stayed in the truck.

Satan is desperate. Through the atrocities in my mind plus the attacks, Satan was doing a good number on me. He was mad that he couldn't have my soul -I'd asked Jesus into my life when I was much younger- but he knew that he might be able to do something even better.

He could try to ruin my witness. He would make sure that I never helped someone *else* get saved. What do they say: desperation is the mother of invention? Well, Satan is inventive.

In recently examining this aforementioned 'church' situation I realized how active Satan was in my life for so many years.

He abhorred the thought of me getting built up in the

Lord. He had to keep me from fellowshipping, studying the Word, worshiping God or anything else related to Him.

The devil knew that if I started believing that God cared about me and was able to help me through my troubles (I reiterate, not that He will necessarily take them away, just help you through), I might lead someone else to Him.

God isn't going to shoot you down for missing church or skipping your Bible reading. Just realize, though, that if you never fellowship in *some way* nor read His Word, you probably suffer for it.

You will probably be weaker spiritually, emotionally and maybe even physically. You might make choices you wouldn't otherwise.

You might think that you are to sick to go to church. Drag yourself in screaming and in pain: those there will probably understand just fine. The church is a body of believers who know that sick people need to get better and they know the salve is Jesus.

You might be oh-so-busy which, especially in our current world, makes sense! Don't go missing months on end though and trying to justify it to yourself.

You might think that you're too 'bad' to go: Jesus came for the sick and the 'bad', not the ones that were already well and thought they were righteous.

And don't think that choosing to neglect God is a choice for being self-sufficient because it's not. Neglecting God is a choice to follow Satan, whether you know it or not.

I had been sitting in my current make-shift cell- our truck- for about fifteen minutes, reading a book and feeling a little calmer than before. Suddenly the sound of someone tapping on the window ripped my nose from my book.

Seconds after the initial surprise, I rolled the window down, trying to appear normal, and said, "Oh hi Uncle Barney, what are you doing?" "Oh, I was just going downtown to Ming's for dinner, and I saw you in here. What are you doing?"

He had no idea-heck, few of my extended family members had much of an idea. I mean, they had heard that I might have a little 'nervousness' issue but that was about it.

The whole 'phobia' issue was something that only my immediate family and one or two friends knew about. Those that actually appreciated that I couldn't just 'convince myself out of my fears' was much smaller yet.

To most people, including aunts and uncles, grandparents and cousins, I made excuses: 'I have a leg cramp from sitting too long'; 'I swooned because I got up too fast'; 'I dropped something on the floor and want to pick it up'; 'I have an inner ear infection which makes me lose my balance.'

> *By the way, those were actual excuses I had used at least once, if not more. That was my life, lying to save me feeling embarrassed.

"Where are your mom and dad and the rest of them?" Uncle Barney asked. I replied, "Oh, they're inside the church."

Uncle Barney looked at me and then looked at the church; his glance inquired with a bit of confusion, 'then why are you *here?*'

Trying to connect the dots, he asked jokingly, "Oh, what did you do that was so bad they even denied you the chance to go to *church?*" I laughed.

"Oh no, that's not it. My legs are just really sore and I keep having these bad cramps –must just be growing pains- so mom and dad said I could stay here."

The look Uncle Bernard gave me made it apparent that he knew I was lying. He scrutinized me over once more as if considering whether he should press the issue. He instead pushed away from the truck and said rather stiffly, "Okay then. Well... um, see you later Blaire. I hope that your legs feel better," and left.

I sat in the truck feeling horrible about my pathetic lies.

RAGING SKIES

If my tears were galaxies
The stars would shine brilliantly.
All of my scared thoughts and fears
Would be rainbows
Illuminating my thoughts.
I would sing but not for joy
For the weight of the tears
On my mind
Are too heavy for me to handle.
If the rainbows shone
It would show all of you
The scared me that
You don't see.
Galaxies would collide with
Rainbows
And all beauty
Would be
Gone

SECTION 6: DYING DOGS ON THE SIDE OF THE ROAD

Many days were spent confined to my room, avoiding open spaces/'attacks.' Actually, I don't know if it's called 'confined' since I chose it.

Then I would get these very rare moments of adventurousness. I guess even my warped brain and/or body realized I needed to move. That's when I would sometimes decide to venture out.

****

CHAPTER 28

I'd been seeing a North Battleford psychologist whom I named The Crazy Bird Lady. I didn't name her that out of spite; I actually liked her and she happened to look a little bird-ish. At least she offered me tangible homework to try to get better.

She was into relaxation for anxiety and depression. 'If I had anxiety and also had seizures, maybe the anxiety was just a trigger.' I wasn't sure if I believed it, but it was the best diagnosis I'd yet heard.

At one session, she'd given me relaxation tapes... and instructions to deep breathe and picture waterfalls and green blue pools or something.

So one grade eight day, armed with the tape -there was definitely no Bluetooth or CD players invented yet- I went out to conquer the world (well, something like that). I also had a book – "Chicken Soup for the Soul"- to read. And the stool that I was going to sit on in the middle of the pasture behind my house.

When I wasn't reading the book, I would do the calming techniques on the tape. I figured that sitting in such an open space would be somewhat alarming, which was where I'd put to use the calming techniques I'd learned.

No one else was home save for dad in the shop. I figured that if I screamed in panic in the pasture, no one would hear me and therefore I would not be embarrassed.

*

On leaving the house I felt a fresh, warm breeze blow through my shoulder length brown, wavy hair. I saw the wind gently blow the pages of my book open. I felt the warm sun shine on my skin.

Best of all, I wasn't even self-conscious about the stool and its presence. If someone chanced upon seeing me and asked what I was doing I could tell something close to the truth.

It's not totally nuts to sit in a field and read (I don't think). The plausibility of the story I would ever possibly have to tell added to my near exuberance.

When I reached the shop I heard dad welding. Just a few feet from the entrance I called and waited for him to appear. After a minute he came out of the shop. My stool and I were two feet away from him; I left it standing there and went over to see him... alone.

Looking at me askance he asked suspiciously what was the matter. In answer, I crossed the couple feet with nothing remotely close to me for support lest I should need it. I reached out my arms, all the while smiling, and gave him a hug (I know it seems totally redundant to mention that I crosses a 2 foot distance but in my life, that was pretty monumental).

I then leaned my head back to look at him, "Oh dad," I sapped, "nothing at all is the matter! It's a beautiful day that God gave us and I'm just here enjoying it!" If dad was not surprised by seeing me out and about, he definitely was when I mentioned God. I didn't do that much anymore.

Dad slowly reiterated what I'd said: "So you figured that you'd come outside... with your stool... which is over there?" Beaming I replied, "I have great plans for the afternoon!" Guardedly he inquired, "What sort of plans do you have Blaire?" I took pleasure in seeing the look on dad's face when I acted so nearly 'normal'.

I wanted to surprise dad so I went as far as to drop my hands from his shoulders and stepped back. I replied, "I, like, am going to take my stool-eo," I really was feeling good, "and go to, like, the pasture behind the trees there and sit on my stool in the pasture and read my book."

With his head titled just a little and an uncertain look on his face he said, "Well you make sure that you enjoy yourself Blaire." He added, "and be careful."

I very soon reached my destination. I stood at the fence on the edge of the pasture. The lady had said to take a few cleansing breaths so I did. I was supposed to then imagine soothing water pouring down slowly; I did so.

When that was all done I shook my arms out and picked up my stool. Off I went to the middle of the pasture. I wished every day was that good.

I spent a good hour there. I went from momentarily freaking out to calming myself with relaxation and visualization (sitting was a lot less scary than walking or standing but I still sometimes panicked).

The thing was, deep breathing didn't ever offer me a long term fix. Don't fall into the trap of thinking that you can fix yourself all by yourself.

A few techniques and tactics like deep breathing and carrying stools won't keep you calm forever. And the moments I felt good were obviously not that good (this day that I was feeling good I still could go little further in open spaces than two feet).

Don't look for temporary fixes that are found within yourself of within things or people, look to the Lord who is the same yesterday, today and forever (Hebrews 13:8).

He will never leave you or give up on you.

CHAPTER 29

It was a May Saturday, nearly the end of grade 8. I was the only one in the house- dad was out in the yard; mom and the siblings were gone somewhere. I decided to take a walk. This was something that I simply did not do. Outside where nothing was secure or stable the way I needed it to be? Outdoors where almost everything was far apart? It just didn't happen.

But that day, for some reason, I thought that I had to get out of my comfort zone. Even with my resolve to leave the house, I was terrified. I wanted to act normal-ish but I just couldn't completely do it. So I grabbed a basketball for help. There were just a few issues: a basketball is not sturdy or reliable –it rolls around the second you put it on the floor or ground. A basketball can't support someone who is falling over and shaking.

Of course, at the time I chose to overlook this. Reason said that a basketball was a horrible help, but my desperation and fear said it was ok. I assumed no one would see me. I was out in the country after all. I thought that this was a baby step on the road to my imminent recovery. Since I wanted *that* more than life, I considered this worth it.

With fear and trepidation, I walked out the door. I stood on the deck stretching and over-all procrastinating. Then, in another uncharacteristic move, I found some gumption, grabbed the basketball and ran towards the steps. My eyes were closed in fear, but I went.

Dad was working on some Texas gates in our shop across the yard. He yelled to me, "Why are you running Blaire and where are you going?" I heard him but I pretended that I hadn't. If I stopped I might never get going again.

I jogged all the way down our driveway. Even the stitches in my side never made me stop. At the end of our driveway, sweaty and completely out of breath, I sat on a nearby rock to rest. After eleven seconds (I counted to distract myself from the open spaces), I forced myself up.

I quickly stretched my arms high above my head, all while holding the basketball in my hands. I jumped up in the air and then purposely hit myself in the head with it three times. I am not making this up. My plan was to go to the pasture because I thought I could handle this.

One thing I liked was the patches of purple flowers in the pasture: focusing on colorful things helped me be less overwhelmed by the spaces around them. The sage green grass was a nice texture which was important to me too. It was not all the same length, which I liked for a reason I understand completely but can't explain.

Thinking of just getting to the pasture, I wasn't aware that there was someone else on the road until I heard his voice. My cousin Delbert was out hauling some bales and I hadn't even heard his truck. Seeing me, he stopped and rolled down the window.

Nonchalantly he said, "Hey, what are you doing with a basketball? You look kind of like a weirdo." I was scared of being found out and terrified of the open space. I was also embarrassed and at a loss for words. Here I looked nuts, was scared, and my thoughts of being alone were only a mirage.

A little too irately I snapped, "Well thanks for that Delbert but all I'm doing is-" and then I paused. I had no idea what lie I could tell him that would make me appear normal. Finally I choked, "I'm practicing bouncing the basketball on the ground and working on my hand and foot work because I'm thinking about joining the basketball team."

I knew right away that I sounded dumb and just imagined him judging me. For some reason that I don't understand, Delbert didn't call me out. He did something worse though, though he probably didn't mean to. He threw me a confused and pitying look and said. "Well okay then, have fun."

With a glance back at me he put the truck into drive and took off. When I was sure he was gone I said to myself out loud, "That was very possibly the dumbest thing you've said in your entire life! You are so transparent! You are taking the basketball to bounce it on the road to practice for being part of the team? Seriously?" –talking to myself was one of my more sane moments.

I saw many psychologists over the years. Only one ever tried to challenge me, though. He'd seen me for quite a while and knew a lot about my tactics and my problems. Feeling he was fighting and losing a pointless battle, he talked to my parents. He said that I did not *want* to get better.

Mom and dad did not tell me about this for many years. Despite the time that had went by, I was infuriated beyond belief when they did. I now see that his diagnosis made sense. I did not completely cause what I had but what I could control, I didn't try to fix.

I said that there was no way that I would have chosen that pain for myself. I sarcastically thought, "Of course I don't enjoy being sick!"

I was listening to Joyce Meyer one day several years ago. She said that sometimes people are hurting so bad –they have great fear or bitterness or whatever the case may be- but they cling to their *problem.*

It is like the problem has become a big part of their identity and they don't want to lose the fear or resentment or paranoia because at least it's *familiar.*

My fear of open spaces was kind of like that. I clung to my pain despite the fact that it was eating me up. Fear may not have been great but at least it was something I knew.

As Joyce also says, "You can suffer the pain of change or suffer remaining the way you are." Sometimes you've just got to say enough is enough and take a leap of faith.

Just recently (in 2019) I realized something. I might not be able to stop each and every 'attack' through faith. I might not be able to stop the terror I feel sometimes in open spaces.

And though all or at least some of our faith may at times fail, God remains faithful. I can trust that God's got me in the palm of his hand.

Trust that circumstances sometimes suck but there's no point in dreading life when God has so much good for me. It's not blind trust either.

He says it in His word and whispers to our hearts. He's in the moments that we can't even explain, He just *is* and your heart knows (Romans 1:19-20). Even if you tell yourself and everyone around you that He is *not,* you know.

When I do trust that God can help me without taking away my problems, things happen.

When I say, "Jesus is Lord" or speak a Bible verse about trust or faith or just about any verse, I sometimes don't have an attack.

The fear and horrible empty feeling of a 'seizure' or 'attack' is there, but I don't crumble.

When I keep moving in trust that God holds me up, I don't fall over or crash into the ground or die like I think I might.

FALL TO THE TOP

There's a Mountain before you
Do you have what it takes?
Can you climb that Mountain,
Scraping and Falling as you go.
Or are you the Person that
Takes the easy way
Around. Look
Deep into your soul.
Who do you want to be?
Glory does not come easily.
But hopefully You don't know
That Yet. You're still
Busy Scraping And
falling

SECTION 7: SPINDLES, SPOKES AND MOONS

There are some things that almost every young North American has, wacko syndrome –to borrow some words from Fabian- or not.

The common denominator is friends. Acquaintances too but when you're a teen, you consider anyone either your friend or your enemy, no grey about that.

****

CHAPTER 30

It was a cool but pleasant mid-October, 1996 day. "So," I said to Chantelle and Teya, while holding my hands on my hips, "do you think that we should give Randy and Jimmy and Robert a call?" Chantelle smiled and poked me in the ribs.

"You just love them, don't you Blaire?!" "I do not love Randy and Jimmy and… well, I can't really say that's totally true for Robert, now can I?"I was having a grand old day sitting around with the girls, relishing the fact that I felt so comfortable at the moment.

We had a very cool (we thought) nickname for the three boys. They were, collectively, the 'Towny Boys.' We thought it sounded like they belonged to us. Some days after school I'd stay in town and the six of us would hang out.

We'd start our time at the school playground and end up in Teya's screened-in porch. With her dad's hunting trophies and mounts all around us, the six of us would sit in folding chairs, holding hands with our respective boyfriends or girlfriends. Or sometimes, before entering the patio, we'd play hide-n-go-seek in the dark outside Teya's house.

I just loved being with the two girls –or three if Danielle came- and the Towny Boys.

> So was I a total fake little kid like Christopher always said?
> Living a pretend life of 'seizures' and terror to get attention
> and out of things I didn't want to do? Then deliberately forgot
> about it all the moment that I was doing something fun?
> Yes, there were a couple of times I could somewhat
> squelch my fears when I felt the need; like I was just fauxing.
> Like holding a baby for instance. I told myself I absolutely
> could not seize at that moment and so I did not. But the fear
> was always there.

*

I had inward freak-outs at Teya's/in Edam with the towny boys every once in a while. It really somehow was generally not that bad. I was calm with them and calm equated to less seizures -though I still was sure I couldn't will them away completely by any means.

That Thursday was not a typical towny day. That day involved two incidents that though mostly unbeknownst to anyone else, were horrible. It started with Danielle, Chantelle, Randy, Jim, Robert and I walking together over to Teya's.

We were walking in the middle of the road. Every Edam teenager I knew walked on the road, not the sidewalks. I was pained and afraid but coping sandwiched between Danielle and Chantelle. I was looking like a good, uneventful arrival.

Suddenly Chantelle and Randy starting play fighting. I couldn't be guaranteed my current life-lines would stay where I wanted them to so I freaked. I frantically pulled Danielle's over to the sidewalk, to a power box adjacent to someone's lawn.

Glaring, she demanded to know what the heck I was doing. I thought hard and fast. There was nothing rational (or true) I could say. So, as was characteristic of me in these moments, I lied: "Oh come on Danielle, wake up already! Don't tell me that you didn't see that too just like how I did."

Danielle had no idea what I was talking about –which made sense because I was making it all up. She sarcastically and skeptically asked, "What was I supposed to see Blaire?" I racked my brain to create the rest of the lie and after a second said, "Oh, don't give me that stupid act Danielle! Like, didn't you see that there was a furry little creature on top of this power box? I just wanted to go over and see what it was, that's all."

Truthfully I did not ever have any interest in seeing a fuzzy animal up close. There was no hesitation before she accused me of being 'such a liar!' She turned on her heel to go back to the road. I desperately said, "Why don't you stay on the sidewalk with me?" Irately she spat, "Why would I want to do that Blaire? The road's nice and fun and open and I'm rather enjoying myself."

I had no choice but to painfully stay alone on the sidewalk. Even more mortifying was that when we reached Teya's, I had to figure out how to cross the street without embarrassing myself. I wanted everyone to go in so I could insanely make my way bit by bit across the street, but I couldn't ask them to do that without giving away my motives.

I realized that I needed help. I motioned Jimmy to me. When he reached me, I grabbed onto his arm and started running across the road. He was so befuddled by me pull-running us across the road that he couldn't speak for a few seconds. After catching his breath he inquired, "So what was it you wanted to tell me?" "Oh gee," I lied, "I forget." He believed me.

*

In her yard, Teya motioned for us girls to follow her. Just beyond the house, Chantelle firmly planted her feet in the ground and demanded what the plan was. We waited for the towny boys to catch up to we girls before Teya mentioned what it was that she had in mind:

Teya sad casually, "I thought that since we play hide-and-go seek in the dark lots, like, how's about we all, like, play hide-and-go seek in the dark in the light?" Randy interjected, "Don't you mean, Teya, how's about we all play *regular* hide-and-go seek." "Yeah," she said, "like whatever."

Jim sidled up to Teya, casually throwing one arm over her shoulder. "I think that's a pretty good Teya, let's all do that guys. I bet it'll be lots of fun." I would rather have choked to death but I only scowled.

I think Danielle was mad at me that day because when she was my horrified face, she didn't console but tried to hurt me. Even though she was one of the few people that knew all of my horrors, she sarcastically spat, "What's the matter Blaire, don't you think that's a good idea?" She had me at a loss for words: "No... I mean yeah, like I mean yes... sure, that sounds good."

I was too shaken up to make a 'battle plan. And without warning, Randy said to hide. Just as I was going to lose it, I figured how to scrape by: Robert. Having a boyfriend was mostly just a way to 'look cool.' In that moment, though, I desperately threw my arm around him and pulled him close to me. I crooned, "Hey Robert, how about you and I go and hide together?"

Jimmy, overhearing our conversation said, "Oh, that's a great idea!" He threw his chin out suggestively towards Teya. To his detriment she just said nonchalantly, "There's no room for the two of us to hide where I have figured out in my head where I want to go, sorry about that one." Jimmy visibly dropped his gaze to stare at his shoes and sadly rested his cheeks on his palms.

"Well I have a good idea for where *we* should go," Robert said, again turning my attention to him. He hadn't forgotten his wonderful momentary gifting. Before I had time to object he pulled me off toward our hiding spot.

*

After one round of hide-and-go-seek, I talked everyone into going inside. The boys plopped onto the couch, talking about dog poop or something equally gross and horrible. We girls went to Teya's room. She showed us her makeup and we discussed whether you should wear eye liner on your bottom inside eye-lid or not.

On returning to the kitchen we grabbed some pop and all seven of us went to the porch. We talked about the things our young teenager minds thought were so interesting: tteenage world domination (not really); when another high school dance should take place; which girl weighed the least and which boy had the most muscle, etc.

It seemed like little time had passed when Danielle looked at her watch and announced that she had to go home for curfew. Soon only Teya, Robert and I were left. He said with a gleam in his eye, "Your Grandma's is on the way to my house so we might as well walk there together."

His suggestion was rational but I and my disease was not. This was not the time I was planning on letting him know. Still, I had to answer him. My mind wouldn't allow for the possibility of us walking *together.* What if I possibly had an 'attack?' I was sure that I would have been embarrassed forever.

I had to say 'no', even if he broke up with me (we were young and immature so this was a real possibility). I pretended to contemplate for a minute before saying, "You go ahead of me Robert, I just want to walk by myself." He looked absolutely crushed, which I felt horrible about.

My pride, though, was young and alive and vibrant and trumped my sympathies.Not becoming embarrassed in front of him was preferable to losing him. Pride is a terrible thing and it's very true that it really comes before every fall.

So, what were my plans for getting back?

Well, there was a toy scooter in Teya's yard that I could 'borrow' to get across the street. Across from Teya's house, there was a power box- the one that I had seen earlier. I would lean the scooter against the box.

Then I would have to rest... and more importantly, work up the courage to keep on moving. I encouraged myself by thinking about the nearby grassy yards and trees; I could hang onto them if need be (to support and distract me of course).

I was also going to grab a stone that I could hold in my hand. Pressing it would help distract me in order to complete the monumental task of crossing streets. Skipping really fast with my eyes closed while whistling was also a good tactic.

I was quite sure there were no vehicles around at that time but if there *was,* I was banking on them not running me over while I skipped and played with a rock and closed my eyes while whistling.

If anyone asked me why I was acting nuts, I would come up with something (I usually did).

CHAPTER 31

There was some teacher thing so school let out early that day in October 1996. Knowing in advance that we'd have a free afternoon, Chantelle had invited Danielle, Bobbi and I over to do French manicures.

When we were all in her living room, she handed out the nail supplies we would need. She gave us a very precise explanation of how to apply the little half-moons to our nails. She informed us that once we had put the strips on, we would paint them with the manicure polish and 'look fabulous.'

"Can I look at the half-moons?" Danielle asked in her inquisitive way and Chantelle passed them over to her. Danielle examined the nail tips and the other girls gabbed. I sat quietly and uncomfortably on the beige couch looking at the beige room and contemplated.

As a teenager with 'panic attacks' I had a different way of looking at things than most of the general public. In empty rooms I would quickly look for little things like pillars or doors or chairs or anything jutting out of what were, to me, the open spaces.

It's not that I meant to do this; that was just my automatic response from the fear that I had grown accustomed to. I had to know where everything was so that in the case I was required to move from the spot I was in, I could do so with as little fear as possible.

I would think of every possible calculation, scenario and variable I could. I didn't even just think of how much space there was between one point on the *floor* to another: the height of the ceiling, the feeling of the weight of the air, everything was considered.

Across from me was a love seat and behind it was a half wall. On it were two pillars, about three feet apart from each other. On the other side was the kitchen. There was a table and chairs and a little farther yet the sink and cupboards.I was formulating a battle plan in the case I needed it.

I was noting to myself where the coffee table and couch were when Danielle interrupted my thoughts. She had finished her examination and looked up, saying, "Okay, I think we are ready to do this. I read the directions and I know what to do."

Chantelle replied, "Of course you know what to do, I told you all before you even read the directions," and she sighed over-dramatically.

Bobbi interjected, "Well, mom is coming to pick me up pretty soon so I'll start by doing Danielle's nails and then she can do mine and same for Blaire and Chantelle."

Everyone agreed to the plan, so Chantelle moved off of the love seat and came to the couch. She brought with her some of the half-moons for us to use. The other two girls settled on the love seat.

"Okay, which hand first?" Chantelle asked me. I wanted to answer but I was still a little lost in thoughts of spaces. When she saw the troubled look in my eyes she whisper-hissed, "Blaire, are you ok?" "Yeah, fine, just a little antsy for some reason.

"I want to, like, get my nails done though so this should be ok." Chantelle shot me a 'you're weird' look. "Okay" she said warily, "Well which hand first then?"

Chantelle was talented at pretty much everything. She flew seamlessly through the nails on my left hand and motioned for me to give her my right. She deftly and swiftly painted all my fingers so they shone beautifully and perfectly. I started thinking that there was no way I could do her nails that fast or that well. Her impending disappointment flooded my mind.

So what did I do? I looked across the room at Danielle and Bobbi to see how their nails looked, hoping that if theirs weren't as perfect as Chantelle's, I wouldn't feel as inadequate. The distance between the couch and the love seat seemed very big. I started to shake a little.

Since I knew an attack was coming on I jumped up, thinking I might stop the inevitable attack from happening if I moved.I lunged at the pillars (missing Danielle and Bobbi who were on the loveseat) and wrecked the beautiful nail job that Chantelle had done.

Chantelle watched the whole escapade in shock that turned into anger. "Blaire, what on earth are you doing?" she near-yelled. I was embarrassed beyond words but at least I felt the familiar, brief feeling of relief of briefly putting off an inevitable 'attack.'

Danielle and Bobbi were also both looking at me like I was nuts. Chantelle threw her hands up above her head. Behind clenched teeth she fumed, "Did it ever occur to you that maybe you are taking this too far Blaire?"

CHAPTER 32

'Mature me' developed an affinity, in September 1996 -the beginning of grade 8- for crutches. This was not like the time in school where I rolled my ankle and needed crutches; I was physically *fine* and I still had them.

I thought that with them 'surrounding me', I would be less likely to have an attack; somehow, I even figured that an attack would be smaller if I had them with me. Absolutely none of this was true but I felt I needed them.

So, one fall mom agreed to my request and got them for me from the Edam hospital (she worked there and could easily rent them).

The day after she delivered them to me, we were scheduled to see one of the many psychologists or psychiatrists that I had been referred to. I can't remember the guy, but I remember his residential office building… or rather, the outside of it.

Danielle and Chantelle had come along with mom and me. I don't know a lot of teens who think it's cool to have their friends hang out with them at the psychiatrist's but I am not normal.

We sat in the backseat of our Dodge truck and gossiped and laughed and had so much fun. There was no room for my crutches so they sat on the front passenger seat beside mom.

We arrived and parked along the sidewalk of the residential office building and I took in the surroundings. There were giant old oak trees swaying in the wind; the inviting lush green grass; the nearby buildings' beautiful brick facades.

When mom prompted for us to exit the truck, I went to grab my crutches. Unfortunately, it was easier said than done; I wanted to grab them while being able to stay in the 'safety' of the truck.

I realized I needed someone to get them and pass them to me; I nominated Danielle. When she got out, she left the back door ajar and I scooted over to the edge of the backseat. That's when it happened.

Just as she was about to pass them to me my face began to freeze. I thought I should get out of the truck right then. I figured a change of position would be enough to halt the imminent 'attack.'

I hopped quickly and awkwardly from the seat to the sidewalk, bouncing on one foot while keeping the other leg high up in the air out in front of me.

Chantelle -who had been the first out of the truck- shot me a weirded-out expression. She inquired, "What are you doing Blaire?"

All the jumping around had momentarily postponed my 'seizure' so I could still speak, "I am just gauging the area, that's all." With my mix of seizures, lies and crutches, I don't know how I had any friends at all.

"Well why don't you grab the crutches and we'll"- Danielle began. She stopped short when she saw the look in my eyes. I began shaking and fell over; Chantelle tried grabbing me before I hit the pavement, but to no avail.

I could distantly hear everyone as if muffled through water. I couldn't see Chantelle beside me but she rubbed my hand so I knew she was there. She was murmuring, 'It's okay Blaire, just a few more seconds.'

Danielle was saying, 'seriously?' somewhere outside of my current vision. I heard mom say, "We got her those crazy crutches like she asked. You'd think we could just walk up to the damn doctor's office without all of this. You know, you want to help someone but this is getting old."

I'd fallen on my back and since I couldn't really move I looked at the sky. I saw the tops of the oaks; I felt the warm, late September breeze. Moving my eyes as far ahead of me as possible, I could see some of mom. Just prior to my attack she'd started walking toward the office. Now she was walking towards us three slowly.

She had a nonchalant and slightly annoyed look on her face. No one seemed too concerned. It made me realize that my life was truly funny in a pathetically sad way.

Until I was twelve I could fall asleep in a vehicle but that ended shortly after the 'attacks' started. Why? *Not sleeping* was one of my 'mechanisms.' It made me 'feel calmer.'

The thought-process went like this: I should only have one 'attack' a day and if I had one, I would be free for the rest of the day unless I slept.

Sleeping was like 'resetting' myself. If I did I might have another seizure; the solution seemed obvious. What I needed more than anything was Jesus in my life. Again, I don't mean that Jesus' *will* is always to take away your earthly problem.

But God never *wills* you to *not* have peace. He never *wills* you to *not* read the Word or pray and by doing so take your eyes off Him.

I should have realized that my problems did not negate the fact that God was with me. I should have given Him every one of my worries.

He would take them away according to His promise in Matthew

11:28.

As Holocaust survivor Corrie Ten Boom said, "There is no pit so deep, that God's love is not deeper still." Isaiah 59:1 says, "Behold, the Lord's arm is not so short that it cannot save; nor is His ear so dull that it cannot hear."

ABANDONED BY YOU

I felt abandoned. But by whom? My brother? He betrayed me a little, he hurt my feelings. I felt I could no longer rely on him and that hurt. But somewhere deep down I understood, even as a hurting kid, his reasons. He couldn't cover for me forever and have a life. He couldn't coddle me and feel respected. He couldn't love me like a brother was supposed to if I was his 24/7 responsibility. I was, after all, his *older* sister.

*

I never felt abandoned by my parents. Mom sometimes drove me nuts but that was all. Dad was maybe a little uninvolved, but I never felt abandoned by him. Nikki never abandoned me- I don't think we had let ourselves get close enough for that to happen anyway.

*

And it wasn't my friends either. Because, despite my screwed-up-ness, I *did* have friends: Bobbi, Danielle, Chantelle, Jenine, Stephanie, Lyndsey, Rhonda, Suzanne, Nicolle, Roachie, Bellanger, Jason and Remi, Larry and a few more (that's not bad for a 'weirdo'). They sometimes got frustrated with me –how could they not when I wasn't even sure if I had seizures or a weird type of phobia- and I with what seemed to be cruelty, but they never had abandoned me.

****

'Abandoned' was the word I reserved for God. I screamed and

cried out to Him, pleading with Him to heal me... or even strike me dead but just to end the agony.

I begged for Him to get the doctors to forget their agendas and appearances and how it made them look to not know the answers. He could have helped them want to search until they found the right answer, but He never. I begged for the right diagnosis and then, of course, treatment but the pain just droned on.

I thought that if He loved me and adored me and was *for* me, He would obey me. Since this hadn't happened He must have abandoned me. I had faith in His abilities (wavering and confused faith, but still faith). I never realized that my pain could be part of a plan that God had (Jeremiah 29:11). And not a plan ONLY to further the gospel but to make my life EVEN BETTER.

Jeremiah chapter twenty-five God speaks through the prophet. Israel has turned a blind eye and a deaf ear to Him. They have turned to their own ways, leaving their first true love. *God has been abandoned.* He misses them, He yearns for them, and He pleads for them.

Their punishment is not from Him, it is from them. It was the price they exacted on their own heads. It was a necessary and inevitable consequence of *their* actions, not God's. The Israelites were told in Jeremiah 25 that the consequence of their actions was a 70-year captivity in Babylon. I also chose '70 years captivity in Babylon'.

I chose, not God. My disastrous life was a consequence of my own actions. God said, 'obey me uncompromisingly.' Even if I didn't understand Him, He said for me to trust Him. I chose not to obey; I chose to go my own way. *I* abandoned *God.*

My health problems were something genetic or something like that, not God's doing. But it could have been part of what God would use... if I would let Him. But I couldn't even imagine something like that.

******

When you feel too scared to trust, ask for help to trust. When you feel faithless, ask God to give you faith. When you feel that you can't stand, ask Him to not only stand with you but hold you up.

When you fall on your face like I did, it might be because you walked away from Him and in the process, you fell. Don't think you're abandoned by God, because you're not. If you're feeling alone, check how far you have moved away.

DISGUISED

One has gorgeous blonde hair and blue eyes
That she uses as her Disguise;
Never revealing the person inside,
A smile on her face is how she hides.
Another excels at all she's been taught,
So Disguising her feelings with a mind always wrought,
 She gives no attention to anything but school,
She Disguises and hides the inside fool.
And he Disguises himself with the Mask of Class Clown,
Only when no one's looking does he show his frown,
No one notices when he is sad
And no one will with the Disguise he has.
But the small child who plays on the floor,
Is the one who really knows more.
If only his innocence could keep him this way
But as he gets older it will be lost one day,
And then only at last is the end of denial
When the real them they show is stated "senile",
And still no one will notice that they're showing the real them
And it will be passed by, they will die, it will start over again.

SECTION 8: NOTHING

LOONEY TOONS IN STORAGE- APRIL 15TH 1999

The school bus has come and gone with Fabian and Nikki but I feel too horrid to join them. I am scared to walk to the bathroom to just get *ready* for school, let alone *go*. So now Mom, dad and I stand in the kitchen.

I don't know how I got to the kitchen, but I did. I guess that with the bus gone, some of the pressure is gone momentarily (if you don't get it, I'm sorry). I immediately stand by the table, screaming and crying about my horrible life. The first one to speak -besides me screaming and whining- is mom: she says that maybe they should keep my pills for me, "...so you don't have to worry about it."

I am taken aback because I don't see how that remark has anything to do with my frenzy. Though he hasn't spoken, I look to dad. I plead, "What is wrong with me? Why do I never get a moment's peace? No one —not the doctors, not the psychiatrists- have any hope for me. You don't say it, but I know you have no hope for me getting better either.

"I am getting older and older and how am I going to be able to leave home? I am going to be confined here forever! You know you hear about, like, circular reasoning and stuff?" I don't think dad knows what I am talking about so he shakes his head and waits for me to explain.

I moan, "Well, you know how when someone who believes the Bible says that the Bible is true just because the Bible says it's true? That's circular reasoning, right? Well, everything is like circular reasoning for me except there's no reason to anything! Like, okay, here is the thing. I have these 'attacks' or whatever they're called.

"Maybe I started being scared of having attacks because I go in open spaces and then maybe since when I have to go in open spaces I have attacks and become more scared of open spaces and have attacks in them. That's my circular reasoning that doesn't have any reason to it, like, at all!"

"Oh Blaire," mom says and puts her arm around me, then moves to face me. I scream to them both, "I absolutely hate my life! Nothing can possibly be worse than my life! No one could ever have felt worse than I do, no one could have felt fear like I do, no one can feel as alone as I do, no one can be as misunderstood as I am, and *no* one could be as frustrated as me!"

Mom casts her eyes at the floor and shifts a little closer to dad. She looks a little constipated to tell you the truth- I have to stifle a laugh, even amidst my tears. She clears her throat and croakily addresses me, "Blaire, we understand that you have never felt worse than you do now. You are terribly depressed and"- mom puts her hand over her mouth and turns her face away.

Dad obviously feels, though, that whatever mom started needs to be said so he continues for her: "You know your pills...." With my fingers tightly intertwined in my hair, stuck in a pose of abject despair, I manage a look up. I am dumbfounded as to why he would mention my pills and shriek, "What are you even talking about dad?"

"We never really... I mean.... Oh, well, here's the thing Blaire. You know how you keep your pills in your room and take them every day?" He very uncharacteristically bites his lip and pauses. After a few seconds he says, "Maybe you have enough to think about without having your pills in your room." "So, you're saying..." but I choke on the words.

I chew on the skin around my index fingernail until I am composed enough to keep speaking, "So you're saying that you want to take my pills away from me?" This is an intensely touchy subject for me, which dad realizes. He steps forward and rubs my arms before saying, "Only because we think it might help you."

"This isn't about helping me," I say with defeat, "Don't you think that I know what you are doing? You don't trust me and..." but I stop talking, at a loss. Mom answers for him, saying, "No, we know that you do a very good job with your pills Blaire, even Dr. Lory always said how mature you were with medical things."

I cut her off, "You want to talk to me now about Dr. Lory and you possibly think that, like, talking about the guy who has almost single handedly ruined my life is a, like, good idea?" She replies, "He hasn't ruined your life Blaire," mom begins to say in his defense. Dad cuts in, seeing that a discussion about Dr. Lory will not end well.

"Blaire, this is the crux of the matter. You want the truth so we'll just tell you. You are so distraught –which we do not blame you for at all- so we think that having your medication in your room is dangerous. What if one day you just feel so horrible and see those pills sitting there and you think...." He doesn't finish, but we all understand.

Incredulously I inquire, "Is that what you think dad?" I quit crying, so shocked am I at this completely foreign concept. "Well honestly Blaire,what if...?" I cut him off, "No dad, not 'what if' anything. You seriously think that I would attempt to commit suicide? Why would I even dream of that?"

"Blaire, I've heard you in your room, screaming that you just want God to let you die." "Yes dad, you have heard me say that,"

I say in a horrified voice. I nod my head dramatically and say, "I would *love* for God to just let me die. But I would never even dream of taking matters into my own hands and-" I compose myself a little and say,

"I don't have anything in my life that I control mom and dad, nothing except my pills pretty much.If you take them away from me then what I thought I'd never do, *that* is when I might think about it but I still don't think so because I just, like, never would!"

Mom steps closer to me, puts her arms around me and hugs me long and hard. When she pulls back, dad says possibly the most important words of my life up till this point:"Blaire, God says that He will never give you more than you can handle." I am not sure where he is going with this.

I am going to whine that I can't handle anymore but Before I can protest dad continues, "And I realize that you may have basically all you can handle, Blaire. He might have given you so much that you can't handle anything more but He'll never give you more than that without giving you a way out.

"I don't think that you can possibly get any worse than you are right now. You are at your rock bottom, the end of your rope. I am not going to sugar coat it or lie to you, that's how it is." With sad humor in my voice I say, "So this is supposed to be making me feel better dad?" Ignoring my comment, he continues, "God will *absolutely never* abandon you."

Draw a line from one end of a page to the next. One starting with a vertical notch on the left for an earth birth and less than a millimeter later, another for death.
The line that continues on to the right signifies eternity in

heaven or hell. This line is not stopped by a notch on the right. Eternity goes on indefinitely.

I told one of my sons that our lives on earth are really miniscule. Our time in heaven or hell afterwards is eternal. I said that the 80-average years we're on earth is a poof of dust in comparison.

In 1 Peter chapter 1 he is talking about those who will eventually go to heaven after they endure earth.

In 1:6 he says, "In this you greatly rejoice, even though now for a little while, if necessary, you have been distressed by various trials."

Maybe you are thinking that Peter doesn't know what a trial is. If that's the case you need to stop yourself.

Pain is sooooo easy to get caught up in (I know!) that it is hard to see anything other than your hurt.

Know that there is an end and that end might come sooner than you think. Even if it doesn't, remember that life is a blink.

If your trial keeps going longer than you expect, at least hold on to the one who is able to see your whole timeline.

Maybe some of the things that I told my kids, if they'd been told to me, would have helped me. I very much doubt it though. Or maybe they were and I never paid attention.

We all often have great ideas of how things would have gone... in hindsight but we don't have foresight.

You don't know the future. Don't waste your time burning bridges before you get to them because you're too scared to relinquish your limited life to the one who DOES have foresight and hindsight and every other kind of sight possible.

Dad's words aren't super insightful or anything, but I believe him. I feel a sort of peace that I haven't felt in a long time. Sure, I am still crying and going insane, but for the first time in a long time, I have the impetus to take baby steps back toward God, to trust God.

Dad doesn't tell me that 'God loved me so I could handle anything.' He doesn't quote Bible verses like, "I can do all things through Christ who strengthens me" nor, "I have come that they might have life and life more abundantly."That is the best thing though. His simple words are what I need to hear: God hasn't and isn't going to leave me.

He doesn't *not* care about me. Even that there might be a purpose to my pain. Not that God causes my sickness, but that He might use it but not use me, if that makes sense.

Jesus died on the cross and in doing so, took our sin upon Himself (everyone's, present and future). God had to turn His face from His own Son because the sin that Jesus took onto Himself for us was *that* horrid. God knows agony and He is there with you for yours. If you trust Him –even though it seems hopeless- you will find that His strength will be yours.

His heart breaks because your heart is breaking.

To fix everything would be erasing the fact that we chose to sin with the free will that God gave us since He loved us so much as to lets us choose even when it hurt *everyone*.

YELLOW BRICK ROAD–
MAY 3RD 1993

Around 2:00 a.m. on May 3rd I am jarred awake- breathing hard, fear resounding in my head, my right leg doing a shake-spasm type of thing. This is not welcome at all. Well, none of my 'attacks' are, but so far I've not had any at night.

I try to remember if the dream that I had had while sleeping was about open spaces; if so, the fear it caused might have triggered an attack. Though this is not a good new development, maybe it is nothing too serious.

Then I have another attack and I become very scared and very confused, very quickly. When it is over I sit up and just wait. Several uneventful minutes go by so I decide to sleep. While still contemplating, I have attack number three. This one lasts longer than the first and I am terrified.

I need to get help but I am too scared to get out of my bed. I am worried I might have an 'attack' and fall on the floor and get hurt- this rarely happens but right now that never crosses my confused mind. I wait for one minute and nothing. Then five more. I have finally made up my mind that I will get out of bed to get dad's help when my tired eyelids begin closing....

*

My alarm clock reads 3:30 AM. I was dreaming about walking a yellow brick road with my friend good Danny when I am woken by another 'attack'- number four in this less-than-two-hour space. The second it is over I jump out of bed and walk -but not run- down the hall.

I knock on mom's and dad's door and I call, "Dad, can you come here, I'm having quite a, like, problem." Dad opens the door to me standing there in my Tweety bird night gown. He looks me up and down but I look just fine. I hear mom's voice from her bed saying, "What is the matter Paul?" Turning only his head to mom he replies, "Well, I'm not sure yet but you don't worry about it Elaine, just go to sleep."

Dad knows that quick, unexpected movements freak me out. Considerately he says, "Blaire, I'm going to take your arm now and close the door so mom can sleep." Not many other people forewarn me about things like this. He gently pushes me backward a step, grabs the door handle, pulls it shut and leads me to the kitchen.

At the table he asks, "Okay Blaire, what is going on?" I explain to him what began at 2 a.m. and is still happening. "Blaire, tell the truth: has this happened in your bed before? Have you been woken up in your sleep before to find yourself having an attack?"

"No, of course not and I have been thinking about this. Like, I been listening to these wacko smacko neurologists for years telling me I just have something wrong with my head like a phobia of open spaces or something. Then I have to listen to some other quack psychologist tell you guys that he thought my only problem was that I didn't actually want to get better as if that's true.

"With all of this s**t do you seriously think that I would, like, think still that I have some anxiety problem? I'm not anxious in my sleep dad, I'm not. My dreams are a little freaky sometimes and I can't even get away from open spaces then, but I'm not anxious enough to have 'attacks' triggered by those open spaces.

"To he** with those stupid psychologists and psychiatrists and all that crap, I don't have some mental disorder, this doesn't make any sense! Why won't any of those doctors listen to me, these are seizures! The doctors need to"- but that is as far as I get because attack number five comes just now.

"Are you scared right now Blaire?" I think about it for a minute and then with certainty say, "No. But am I worried? He** yes, I am worried out of my mind!" Dad looks a little confused and somewhat skeptical. It's sad I know this about myself and even sadder to admit, but I'm a bit of a drama queen.

"So, if you were to parade around the entire kitchen you wouldn't be scared of the open spaces?" I laugh sarcastically –because, even in the middle of the bleak situation, it is comical that we talk like we do and have learned to almost consider it normal.

Dad chuckles and just says, "You might as well try to sleep some more Blaire. We'll see if your shaking has gone away after a few more hours. I haven't been in bed for long when I find myself drifting to sleep again, but sleep isn't to be. From 5-ish until 6:30 I have what seems to be one attack on top of another. I know the time from looking at my alarm clock.

*

Now I can hear mom and dad in the kitchen talking. Oddly, my attacks start to slow considerably. A little later I hear Nikki stir and a few minutes later Fabian comes up the stairs from his room in the basement. He knocks loudly and after I grunt, "Yeah," Fabian pushes my bedroom door open.

As soon as I say 'enter', he flips the light on. I screech as I squeeze my eyes shut, "Do you think you really had to turn the light on like that Fabian?" Without missing a beat he says, "I just heard mom and dad saying something about how you're losing it again, thought I would check it out."

I am in no condition to even be thinking about being mean to anyone, but Fabian just pushes my buttons. I retort, "Fabian, why don't you take your sarcastic little @$$ out of here and go jump off a cliff and make sure it's a high enough cliff that you die while you're at it?"

Fabian doesn't say anything to me but just turns off the light and yells to the kitchen, "Well I guess it's another day that she's not going to school, hey mom?"

*

Dad tells me –one of the times he pops his head into my room to see if I am still convulsing, which I am- that after the bus comes he will take me to emergency in Edam. When I hear the bus come and leave, I get out of bed. I get dressed and then make my way rather awkwardly to the kitchen.

Dad asks if I feel any better and in reply I start seizing again. As my thirty-five second 'attack' ends, dad says, "So this has been going since three or so, hey Blairesy?" Dad looks at mom and she says, "Well Paul, I guess you guys had better go."

*

Dad is about to help me to his truck when Roy shows up. Roy is dad's friend and on-and-off hired man. With a change of usual work plans, the three of us get into dad's old Toyota truck. Dad drives and Roy sits shot-gun. Rather than sit between them I choose to sit in the back. Roy folds his seat forward and I crawl into the tiny, cramped backseat.

The backseats don't even face forward- when in the unused position the seats aren't even really seats but things that fold up against the wall. The backseat is so squishy that I think that I may be unable to even *have* an 'attack'.

In 1998 or so dad bought a white Toyota from a guy who had already had the truck for a few years.

> Dad drove that Toyota around everywhere and was not
> rough on it exactly but he was not gentle either.
> Still, it never needed much more than an oil change all
> those years. Several times dad talked about how well engi-
> neered it was; of course, his wording was a little more
> technical!
> He had the Toyota for many years before he sold it to an
> Edam man named Joe. Joe drove it for years and years before
> he finally got himself a new little red truck- not, I think,
> because the Toyota was wrecked but it probably was a little
> bit ratched by that point!

Getting out of the truck at the Lady Minto Health Care Centre
in Edam, I have an 'attack.' Roy awkwardly holds my arm so I don't
fall onto the pavement. After what seems like forever but I am sure
was less than a minute, the three of us get me inside the hospital
where we see a face I will always like- Dr. Dewitt's.

I feel myself standing up straighter on seeing the doctor. I'm
pretty comfortable with him and seem almost happy as he shakes
my hand. He says jovially and with a joke in his voice, "Well what
could be wrong? Because you seem okay to me. I think that I should
just send you home."

I think his comment is kind of funny and I'm about to answer
when my countenance unexpectedly and without my permission
changes. For years Dr. Dewitt has heard about my 'attacks' but till
now he's never actually seen me have one. He is aware, though,
that my Saskatoon neurologists deny or at least doubt that I have
seizures.

When the 'attack' is over he says placidly, "That was not just a
figment or creation of your imagination, was it Blaire?" I shake my

head 'no.' Then Dr. Dewitt grabs his stethoscope, checks my heart and proceeds to check all my other vitals. With his hand around his mouth- perplexed- he begins saying something but is stopped by another 'attack.'

When it is over he says something I've never heard a doctor say: "What do *you* think Blaire?" I slowly focus my eyes on the doctor. I guffaw, "Did you really just say that?" Hesitating –because it's obvious he isn't sure what I mean by *my* question- he answers, "Um, yes Blaire, what do you think?"

I clasp my hands to my chest and motion to everyone in the room –especially my dad. I say in a loud voice, "Just for the record all of you peoples, Dr. Dewitt just asked me a question that no doctor has asked me *ever* in regard to my shaking. He asked me what *I* think."

"So" -and here I turn to Dr. Dewitt- "I am going to answer your question. For some reason, several years ago, I, like, would start shaking when I stubbed my toe or did something like that. I got mom to take me to a neurologist -not totally true- to treat me for seizures –I used to have them so I thought I was just having a little different kind of seizures now.

"The neurologists said that they had never seen seizures like my attack things are like, so they told me that I just had a mental disease and sent me to psychologists. I'm kind of like a hot potato. Everyone seems to want to pass me off. I think that what happened is that my seizures started happening in open spaces so then I became scared of open spaces and then I'd have a seizure there.

"So, then I was more scared and all that. Yes, I realize that sounds like a mental disorder but wouldn't anyone have a mental disorder if they were having seizures in some certain place for some reason? The bottom line is that I have seizures and there's no getting around that. My seizures might look a little, like, atypical or whatever you call it but they are seizures."

Dr. Dewitt doesn't say anything for a second. Finally, and carefully he remarks, "Blaire, I do not have your EEGs, I do not have your MRIs," at which my heart sinks. I am certain he is going to tell me that he disagrees with me, just like every other doctor I've seen.

He continues, "But I do think that you might not have the mental disorder the doctors think. I think that maybe treating a physical illness with psychotherapy might not have been helping you," at which I smile. He limits my jubilee by holding out his palm to me in a motion that says 'just hold on' and says, "I don't know yet if they're seizures but I am going to find out." I am beyond ecstatic that someone might consider what I think.

"What medication are you on right now Blaire?" Dr. Dewitt asks. Dad says, "Tegretol, she's on a medication called Tegretol." "What is it for? I mean, of course I know what Tegretol is generally used for but what reason did the prescribing doctor give?" I say, "Panic attacks and phobia and anxiety." Then Dr. Dewitt says something that terrifies, but also thrills, me: "Take her off of it." And so begins my stay at the Lady Minto Health Care Centre.

I feel that this is the end of the beginning of something- or maybe the beginning of the end of something.

*

I follow one of the nurses to the hospital room that is to be my 'sanctuary' while I am weaned off Tegretol and observed by Dr. Dewitt. I'm missing school. And I might not be in a hotel but it's pretty cool. My room comes with a cool bed that tilts up and down at the press of a button; I have a personal bathroom in my room; there are tables, chairs and a TV in the corner!

And I really like that in this sterile hospital I am the person of interest. Best of all, all-in-all, my normally present fear has been halted somewhat by my current dilemma... and the novelty of having me around -being happy to be in the hospital for attention's sake *does* sound like I'm making up the seizures and fear but I swear I'm not.

I'm starting to think that being off Tegretol might not be so bad after all. I even go so far as to think to myself that 'maybe while observing me, the doctor will realize exactly what is wrong with me. Maybe it'll be so obvious that he would have picked it up if he was my doctor years ago instead of stupid Dr. Lory- and give me the right meds or whatever and I'll be just like any other kid that ever lived.'

There is no foreboding in my mind.

> Probably the worst baggage that I brought into my marriage and still carry is my control issues. I will preface that by saying that I don't really care what anyone else does, just don't touch me unless I ask.
>
> I reference Joyce Meyer often because God has given her wisdom to comfort (not comfort by offering hollow words of sympathy but to really help people take hold of their lives with God's help). With that in mind I will reference her now. God is in control of most everything (meaning He can do just about anything which almost every Christian knows). Though He partially decides our destiny, how that happens partly depends on us only.
>
> It is *not* only up to God how long our tests and trials take, we have a big say. Our choices affect whether we get through that trial quickly or fight it as hard as we can and end up spending years in a valley that could have taken days to walk through.

For years my life felt out of control so those things that I could dictate, I did. I chose who to love and who to forgive and when. I chose when to read my Bible and basically when I went to church. Some days I chose to lie in my bed scared all day and play the victim. I usually even controlled whether I got on the bus and went to school.

The devil wants to ruin you. He wants nothing good for you in any way, shape or form. He wants you to live a horrible life on earth. He wants to deceive you to turn away from asking God to be part of your life.

He doesn't want you to give God control because he knows that is his cue to LEAVE your life (James 4:7). When you let Jesus have control, you're actually being the most pro-active participant in your life that you can be.

The Bible says, "You [who have not chosen Jesus] belong to your father, the devil, and you want to carry out your father's desires.

Satan was a murderer from the beginning, not holding to the truth, for there is no truth in him. When he lies, he speaks his native language, for he is a liar and the father of lies." (John 8:44).

If you have not become God's child it is not because you can't, it is because you won't. It does not matter one iota whether you have been abused as a child verbally or physi-cally; it does no matter if you murdered hundreds of people; it does not matter if you have been a terrible liar; it does not matter if you have bed-hopped like no one's business.

It does not matter if you are in the *middle* of doing any of those things. Just say, 'enough!' None of it dictates whether you can be made new or if you can become God's child.

James 2:10 says: "For whoever keeps the whole law and yet stumbles at just one point, he is guilty of breaking all of it."

Understand that, mediate on that, don't you dare forget that! If you have even committed one tiny sin in your life, it's like you've committed them all.

If you told one little lie, in God's eyes, you are no more sinless than the guy who has raped 15 children.

Romans 3:23 says, "For all have sinned and fall short of the glory of God." No one is worthy to get into heaven on their own merit.

But God loved the world so much that He sent His only son to die on the cross, bearing the sin of the entire world past, present, and future.

If we accept Jesus' offering of Himself as eternal sacrifice for our sins we can one day enter sinless Heaven with spotless God (John 3:16).

Nothing is a license to hate those who have hurt you (and yes, I understand how hard this is). By doing so the person that you are hurting most is yourself and you don't deserve that.

Jesus coming into your life doesn't make the past hurts disappear but He can help you heal!

What you did in the past is non-existent to God "if you confess your sins He is faithful and just to forgive you your sins and cleanse you from all unrighteousness" (1 John 1:9)

MYRNA SMYRNA PEGGERMAN FOOT AND KIRCHHEIM VON KNEE –MAY 4th, 1999

It is May 4th, 1:00 P.M., a school day (but obviously I'm not there because I'm in the hospital) and Danielle walks into my room. Incredulously I ask, "What on earth are you doing here? Shouldn't you be at school?!"

Flippantly she replies, "School? I guess I thought this was much more important than trig." I can't believe that teacher's pet, perfectionist Danielle, is skipping... for me.

Mom and dad have been in my room for close to an hour now. When they see that Danielle and I want to visit, they turn to leave my room for a brief break: "Well we'll leave you two girlies for a while. We're going to try to catch Dr. Dewitt."

Once the door has closed behind them I sit up in my bed. "So, what's all going on at school?" Danielle looks surprised at the thought that in the midst of wires and machines, I want to chit chat. Then she gets a mischievous glint in her eye, "Oh, well you would have loved to see this.

"Today we got Ms. Formanek on the topic of that picture called

'The Wall of Fire.' It's in the parliament building or whatever. We spent the whole class talking about whether they should have wasted however much money on it!" I am so happy to just sit here and veg with Danielle: "You know, Danielle, as much as I, like, love Ms. Formanek and everything"-

"Oh yeah," Danielle cuts in, "the kids in our class and then Danny and the other grade 12s made you some get well cards," she pauses and looks around. She walks over to her bag, grabs the cards and starts coming back to my bed. I start to swing my feet over to the side of my bed.

Danielle quickly stops me and says, "Are you sure you should be not lying down Blaire?" "Oh yeah, it's all good," I answer nonchalantly but sit sideways on the bed, just to ease her mind. Danielle makes me feel grounded and semi-normal. She is interesting and quirky and geeky in her own way –just like me- so I don't want to make things hard for her.

Sitting on my bed, we flip through the cards, laughing at some and almost crying at others. "I don't know why you say you don't like" such and such a guy, she says, "by what he wrote on the card I think that you should drop your Spiritwood boy toy and run away with him."

Danielle takes out some cards from my classmates too. When I see what Stephanie wrote I said, "I could tell her writing from a million miles away!" We both laugh and laugh. Steph is awesome, another true friend (with very recognizable hand writing).

Then though I still want to look at more cards, I halt suddenly. I just can't help it; there I am, lying on my back on my pillow, having a seizure.

*

"I knew that I shouldn't have let you turn sideways Blaire, I knew it!" She is just about to press the call button when I somehow shake my head 'no' (even during my seizure). She slowly pulls her finger away. The seizure only lasts another five seconds –another short one.

Danielle says, "What the heck is wrong with you Blaire? Scaring me like that I mean." A big smile -oddly inappropriate for the moment- breaks across my face. "And what the heck are you smiling for, do you think that any part of this is funny Blaire? I should just go home and spend some good quality time with my Wonder mom and Master Kirk."

Why am I smiling? Because I am having freakin' intermittent seizures but I am busy thinking about how good of a friend I have. I'm sure she'll always be my bestest best friend. She has got to think so too, I'm just sure of it. So though I don't say what my smile is about. Danielle probably knows.

Clasping my hand like blood brothers for life, a smile breaks across her face too. She says, "You know Blaire, no matter what happ-" She never gets to finish because in walk mom and dad. I quickly position myself with my back on the bed and Danielle stands beside it; that is the end of that.

WILL THAT REALLY CUT THE ICING? – May 6th, 1999

It's 9:22 a.m., May 6ᵗʰ, 1999- a very special morning for me indeed. I expect something different today... something good. It's my Sweet 16 and even in the hospital, this is exciting.

Mom and dad stop in around 10:30 and wish me happy birthday. I find myself trying to glance around the doorway after they enter my room, expecting Fabian and Nikki to be with them. Sure, it's a school day but they might show up for an hour and it might be nice -but they're not there.

Mom and dad say they have a gift for me that they'll give me when I get home. I'm not big into special days, but I kind of would have expected a little more for this *particular* day. Then, after only about half an hour, they say they have to go.

Dad has to work and mom has to go to the nurse's desk to get something she left there the other day -mom works here, besides for this week of course. Then she has to go home and do something.

The fact that mom and dad have left so quickly -as if they don't care about me- has doused all thoughts that anything exciting will come of *this* day. I do pretty much nothing for several hours. There are some soaps that I watch in the morning, even though soap operas are dumb.

Anita –a nurse and mom's friend- stops in to say happy birthday and give me a turtle lamp. This, actually, is the most exciting part of this day. I love turtles (something mom must have told her at some point). At least someone gave me something.

Then I'm back to doing more of nothing. The only party I'm going to be getting this day is the pity party that I'm throwing for myself. It's 3:22 PM and I haven't even brushed my hair.

A couple of minutes later I hear a bunch of voices and a knock on my door. Maybe it's the doctor and nurses back; maybe I've been convulsing and not even realized it.

'Man,' I think, 'my life is really pathetic' but before I have time to carry on the thought, the door flies open and in fall about 11 of my friends, followed by Nikki and mom holding her Tupperware cake container. Everyone is talking to me and wishing me happy birthday and telling me they're happy to see me.

Jamie says "Hey, where's the cake at?" which for some reason makes me nostalgic. My cousin Diana, who is a year younger than Nikki, is there and I wonder where the other three –Delbert, Shane and Dustin- are. Still, I am happy to see her cute little face.

Though everyone looks excited to see me, almost everyone seems hesitant to go too close to me or to hug me –like I'm made of glass or something. This is the case for everyone, anyway, except Danielle and Chantelle. They jump towards me and hug me; everyone else's hesitation dissipates.

Danielle hands me a card with a picture of grapes on the front. It says something corny but it so encapsulates Danielle's and my friendship. She says that she will give me a present later but when I get out of the hospital because that is "my incentive." She does, though, hand me a tube of red lipstick –why she got me that I'll never know- and tells me to put some on.

Chantelle passes me her present. It is a box that says something like, "For girls' eyes only." I open it and see a place to store love letters and the like. Chantelle and I are so goofy… and boy-crazy. Chantelle also hands me a cord with a scented, glow-in-the-dark vial to go around my neck. I slip it on and feel invigorated (weird choice of words, I know, but it's true).

Marv, a guy born a day before me but who is not in my class, says that he is happy to see me. We aren't that close, but we share a weird born-a-day-before-me-and-in-the-same-hospital bond; I smile and am genuinely happy to see him. I look over and see Danny, his brother and my best guy friend.

He was once going to go to North Dakota to pick up some cows; he said he'd be gone for two days. I told him that I'd miss him so much.He said that he wasn't sure if he could leave because he'd miss me too much too. I think he went anyway, but we joked that we were such inseparable friends that we couldn't be away from each other for forty-eight hours.

When all that hugging is over I look over and see that Randy -Towny boy Randy- is there. Jimmy and Robert are missing but they tell me he'll be by later. We haven't been anywhere near as close as we were a few years ago so this makes me very happy.

Teya and I are also now not great friends, but I'm happy to see her there too. She says, "how you doing girl?" and we laugh. She always says things like that.

Then before I know it's happening, Lyndsey and Bobbi crash onto my bed, saying that everyone needs to get out of the way because I have to see them. They pull Nikki onto the bed too and the five of us group hug. It feels familiar and loving and wonderful.

I look over and see my drama friend Jenn. I find myself saddened inside. She is great but we don't hang out outside of drama-seeing her reminds me of the fact that I'm in a hospital with serious health issues. 'Probably,' I think, 'she wouldn't be here on a normal day. Maybe a lot of the people here wouldn't be here if they weren't aware of how sick I am and they feel a little sorry for me. Maybe I'm a hopeless case.'

I don't have time to carry on my sad reverie, though, because mom is in front of me, holding her Tupperware cake thing that she's had forever and a day. She pulls the lid off to reveal my cake. The candles are lit and everyone starts to sing happy birthday.

Nikki is still on the bed with me, though everyone else has backed up a little bit. Mom is coming through, holding her Tupperware container. Danielle has mom's camera in her hands- mom handed it to her in order for Danielle to take a picture of her, Nikki and me. I put my arm around Nikki and she puts hers around me: I feel 'close' to her.

Mom motions for everyone in the room to join me on my bed for a picture. So, with the sheets crumpled up; girls and guys everywhere; me with my red lipstick and vial necklace on; me and Nikki hugging (a true, rare sight), mom snaps a picture of us.

It's funny how, on seeing that picture now, I remember that one of the worst times of my life was also one of the best.

I remember little Nikki and her floppy, Mexican-patterned hat.

I remember my vial (and the scent), the red lipstick, my orange hair that I thought was auburn and the shirt I wore that day.

I remember Danielle's pretty face and how she somehow had ended up holding the Tupperware container.

I remember Chantelle and her crazy curls and belly shirt.

I remember Bobbi's hair that she was trying to grow out.

I remember Teya leaning over and putting her hand on my wheelchair. I remember Randy's winning, mischievous smile.

A moment frozen in time

MAY THE 4TH BE WITH YOU TIMES 2 – MAY 8TH 1999

It's the evening of May 8th when dad visits me in the hospital. He brings me a Mars bar, we talk and then the most exciting part:. we play Monopoly © ! Usually he won't play because he says he finds it too much like real life. This week he's played it with me almost every night.

We're about three quarters of the way through the game when I knock the iron token off the board and onto the floor. Dad offers to get the piece but I wave his offer off. Confidently I get off the bed and crouch over to get the piece underneath.

All seems well until I stoop to look under the bed and feel an oncoming attack; I tip over onto my back. Dad notices that I am taking extra-long getting the piece. "Blaire, can you see it?" but I can't answer.

Dad leans over the edge of the bed and sees me lying there with both of my legs shaking and my right arm clenching the air. Dad is at my side in a second. In a near-moan he says, "Oh my Blue-Air." With his arm around me, raising my neck off the floor, I can see he worry; this 'seizure' is worse than usual.

When it is finally over dad says, "You know that we have to

tell the doctor, right Blaire? And since I was winning the game and we're probably going to have to call it quits for tonight, it's probably safe to say that I just won." He winks and even in that moment, I feel better.

When the nurse calls him, Dr. Dewitt just says that he'll see me in the morning, and to be good. Then dad kisses me on the forehead. He says, "You'd better just rest now Blaire," and he walks out the door.

I feel very empty and sad. It's not that late but there's nothing much for me to do. I just sit in my bed with the lights as dad left them, on. That is the only thing I *want* to and apparently am *allowed* to do. I pull the covers up on myself and I feel utterly depressed.

It's not that I miss my boyfriend who hasn't visited since I've been here; he's not that awesome and the fact that I even have one should make me feel not too much of a weirdo. I don't miss my friends nor my parents (that much). I don't even have no hope that I will get better. Tons of people have been in the hospital before and not only not died but gotten better.

I think I am sad because it hurts me so much to see that others -especially dad- hurt so much for me. I mean, he never said it but his eyes belied what he was thinking. I am sad that when it comes to me, no one seems to have any hope.

I begin to cry which turns into sobbing. After a few minutes of this, my Auntie Cami –the LPN working tonight- walks into my room. When she sees me crying she rushes to my bedside."What is wrong?" she inquires genuinely worried.

"Oh, no Auntie Cami, nothing is wrong." I say as I wipe tears from my eyes. I lie, "I just had a fit of sneezing, that's all, and my eyes were watering like crazy which is, like, kind of funny I guess because maybe you won't just have some undiagnosed little convulsing fit kid on your hands, but you might have to feed me some Buckleys too!" I laugh way too big for the moment.

Auntie Cami ignores my obvious lie. She asks, "What's that you've got on your side table? Is that the Bible?" Flippantly I retort, "Oh no, that's an encyclopedia that I found at home in one of the closets- I'm going to learn German. I don't actually have a Bible with me." "Oh, I see. Well, I guess I had better get back out there, I think I hear a bell ringing." She shuts off my light and leaves.

Maybe someone reading this right now likes better to pick up a book –pretty much any book- than the Bible. You might think that the Bible is too old, stuffy and boring to be of any use.

Maybe you don't have a very strong relationship with Jesus –if any at all- so why bother? He's the word (John 1:1, 2 Timothy 3:16) and if you aren't interested in Him, why the Bible? Right?

Maybe you think that you're doing fine. But when you are facing a situation you cannot fix, what are you going to do? What happens when you have no answers? When you're overwhelmed by hopelessness, thinking nothing will ever turn out right?

God wants to help you but He's not going to force His way into your life. Remember the choice that Adam and Eve made? It resulted in something very horrible, but at least they could make choice.

God doesn't want zombies but that doesn't mean He doesn't want you to choose Him. Letting the King of the world –actually, the King of everything- into your life also entitles you to some pretty awesome stuff.

Let me give you an example. Let's say you live in a kingdom but don't know the king. Do you expect he'll show you much personal favor?

If you don't go to the King and you don't make a choice to know the King, why would the King get involved in your life? It's not cruel, he's just not making the choice for you... because otherwise it wouldn't be a choice at all.

*OXYGENATED ELLA-
MAY 9TH, 1999*

I've been at the Lady Minto Health Care Centre for five (or is it six? I don't know whether to count this day since it's not done) mostly uneventful days.I have basically watched TV and read for five days straight.

I have had some great visits.I am even kind of a twisted celebrity (there aren't too many really sick and young people here). Even being weaned off Tegretol actually seems like no big deal since I hardly have any seizures.

I am becoming more certain than ever that Dr. Dewitt will fix me and I will be forever free. My nightmare is ending and I will be able to go home soon. 'After all,' I reason, 'during these five days in the hospital I've had only six seizures and none at night.

My face brightens even more when, skipping school again, Danielle walks in. I tell her there is not much new and we chat a bit. Then we play Monopoly © and I win. She doesn't love the game yet but I will make her a believer!

Grandma LaClare shows up around 3:30. Dani and I both say, "Oh Grannycakes, you're just in time," and then we all watch Wheel of Fortune together. We then spend another few hours doing... well, I don't know... until Grannycakes leaves.

*

Now it's 9:31 P.M. and Danielle is getting ready to leave too. I am in the middle of saying to Danielle that I hope I see her tomorrow when I start seizing on my bed. For a moment I think this is just one of the small, 'normal' seizures I've been having basically all week, the kind I think will go away soon.

A few seconds into the 'normal-ish' seizure. Until both of my legs start shaking. A second later my head falls limp to my side so I can't see all that well. Both of my arms are straight and a little numb and totally useless. This big, horrid, novel seizure has now been going on for at least 30 seconds.

Generally, I can tell when a seizure reaches a climax and is then going to start going down; I am nowhere near that point. Out of my very skewed-at-the-moment peripheral vision I see Danielle standing by my bed but of course I can't talk to her.

She kind of freezes in spot for a few seconds.By the time she runs to the door I've been seizing for at least 30 seconds. Soon a nurse enters my room to see what is wrong. She checks my pulse; now we're at 1 minute, fifteen seconds.

Finally the climax is near (though I still look like a tree with its branches hanging out at odd angles). The nurse says that she is going to call Dr. Dewitt. Danielle should stay there and if the seizure has not ended or at least begun to end in another minute.

*

I am on my 3rd seizure. The first began at 9:31 p.m. and was over approximately three minutes later.The second was a little shorter. It began at 9:38 –Danielle has decided to stay for 'some reason'- and lasted 2 minutes and 14 seconds.

This one, the third, I can feel already slowing and it's only been 1 minute and 43 seconds (I've been counting in my head). When it's done, I find everyone looking really awkwardly at me.

I am uncomfortable in that serious moment that is centered on me, so I try to deflect attention by saying to Danielle,"See, they're getting shorter, it's not so bad. I'm sure these small inconveniences will end soon and I'll be fine." She does not seem convinced.

I go for nearly 20 minutes without another seizure and then... and then it comes. Lying in my bed, mid-sentence with Danielle, I begin convulsing again but much worse than ever before. My whole body convulses; both my arms, both my legs are numb and so is my face. I can feel my shoulder blades pulled together, even though I'm lying on my back in my bed.

Soon Dr. Dewitt walks into my room; I can't see anything because my face is frozen and I don't even know which direction he is but I can hear his voice. He sounds weary- he was probably going to bed when they called. This must be a very sucky part of his job.

A few minutes later my parents arrive, I hear dad say to mom, "We definitely should call Dr. Lory now, shouldn't we?" Mom replies statically, "Oh what has he ever done but misdiagnose her? And then he allowed her to think she is crazy and then send us on a pointless, crazy wild goose chase to psychologist after psychologist. So no, we don't need to phone him just yet."

I have never liked mom as much as at this moment.

*

I would be stretching it a little- but not by a lot- if I said that my seizures, came one on top of another but by 10:25 P.M. I am on seizure number 6. They call the ambulance to take me to the Royal University Hospital in Saskatoon.

I am so exhausted and just want this to be over. Despite all of this, all I can think of is what I am must look like: sweaty hair plastered to a pale face.In seconds I am broken out of my reverie. One can hardly expect to spend more than a few seconds lost in thought while convulsing.

Somewhere in the commotion, the nurses say something about my vitals being good and I think it's great that I'm a seizing kid with a healthy heart.I then find this thought funny and smirk... although

I don't think it looks like anything more than what happens when you're face is frozen so at least no one notices my odd behaviour.

I look to my right and see Dr. Dewitt take out a needle and think that maybe I should ask what it is, but then I realize I don't care. He jabs it into my arm or my hip – I am not sure which because my body seems foreign and kind of distant from me.

Someone comes and sticks something over my face; about thirty seconds later I figure it out that it is oxygen. The person holding the mask, I see when I look up, is Danielle. I am glad she is still there although I am sure she would like to not be... or at least I would like not to be.

Mom's and dad's faces again come into view. I wonder momentarily where Fabian and Nikki are and conclude he must be babysitting. That's another thought that no one in that hectic room would think I am thinking now, but I can't speak so they can't know.

Then I feel the seizures lessen and then stop. And the funny thing is that my eyelids stop working too- they just won't stay open. And it's my mouth too because I can't seem to move my mouth properly *or* stay awake to finish any sentence.

Just before I become oblivious to the world, I hear some-one say, "Valium ©."

*

Someone shakes my shoulder to alert me to the ambulance's arrival to bring me to Saskatoon. I am very groggy from my very short lived 'Valium-induced' sleep; I am told that Mom will be the one to ride with me. The EMTs –I think that's who picks you up to put you in an ambulance when you're seizing?- enter the hospital room and load me onto a stretcher.

I suddenly feel sad again. Something to do with being aware that my problems are big enough to merit me being hauled to another hospital. As we're leaving the room, Danielle and Dad tell me they love me. Mom says goodbye to them and grabs onto the side of my stretcher.

That's when I look over and I see it. Mom's gorgeous, blue star sapphire ring, the one that she only lets me wear about once a year. I realize that in my current state I have a bit of leverage, and I'm about to use it. I give her a really pathetic look –not too hard to do tonight- and then ask if I can wear her ring to the hospital.

She says, as one would expect in this atypical moment, "yes, of course!" I think to myself, 'This just might be one of the best days of my life.' Then I remember that I'm on an ambulance stretcher on the way to the Saskatoon Royal University Hospital.

For the third inappropriate-to-the-situation moment, I laugh to myself.

YOU CAN'T MEET THE QUEEN BUT YOU CAN MEET THE JOKER OF CANTERBURY – May 13th, 1999

I have been at the RUH for three days- or at least I think it's May 13th- but I'm not really sure and I don't really care, truth be told.

The only fun I'm having is admiring my ring that's not really mine –because unfortunately I think I have to give it back at some point.

My seizure problems are real and they are big. Things aren't looking terribly good for me. Of course the doctors here diagnosed me as having epilepsy. I hate that word even though I knew all along I had it: 'epilepsy' sounds about as bad as 'leprosy.'

My life is in ruins. I am hooked up to a bunch of machines to monitor everything. Gauze is wrapped around my head to keep the electroencephalogram attached.

Despite a diagnosis, a solution to my health problems still evades me and everyone else.

***

Four more days go by. They take the wires off. I'm having a bath in a few hours. I haven't had one for a week but I don't really care. I don't foresee *anything* mattering ever again.

Auntie Cami and Suzanne visited; they both cried. I know that it is because they are grossed out by me. They think I'm pathetic compared to their perfect lives. It makes me mad so I don't think about it.

***

It's the 17th: Finally after a week here I am getting ready to go home. Mom's been with me at the RUH all week but now she's gone for a bit. Just to Edam to pick up Danielle and Chantelle who are going to be with me as I leave the hospital.

I think I requested that mom do that for me but maybe she thought of it all by herself. Maybe that's another indication that my life is basically over, like her letting me wear her ring.

I haven't had any grand mal seizures for five or six days. Also, though I never realized this when I was doped up, they started me on some new seizure medication a couple days ago. No doctor really has any hope of it actually working, but maybe it'll do as much as Tegretol did; at least I might not have another grand mal seizure again.

Yesterday I was lucid enough to overhear some doctor tell mom that I'd probably have to live at home forever. He said more after that, but I stopped listening and I think I almost blacked out. I don't think any teenager wants to hear that... ever.

> For years, I hated the Biblical story of Job. I never said that, but I did. I judged God's reasons.
> In my mind, He needlessly and sadistically let Satan tor-

ment Job... but at some point I changed my mind... or maybe God did?

Job began as the picture of true success: he was rich; had seven kids; had a wife. He had many cattle, slaves and servants galore.

Nothing bad ever seemed to come Job's way, everything seemed great. He was religious, upright and blameless.

But there was one thing that I never noticed before that I do now: Job started with

great head-knowledge of God but he never really *knew* Him.

One day Satan pointed out Job to God; God said, 'oh yeah, Job's awesome and reveres Me.'

Satan likes trying to drive God nuts –not that it's ever worked but whatever- so he asked to inflict the things in Job's life. Would Job still praise God then? Maybe God wasn't worth it?

Well, Job lost most of his human possessions –family too- but he didn't curse God. Man, this wasn't working out well for Satan.

So then Satan asked to inflict Job's body with disease and pain. People react most often worse to having their own bodies attacked. Same result.

But... Job kind of says that he is nearly on par with God (31:35-40) asks God not-so-respectfully why on Earth God was doing this. Kind of like, 'what is wrong with you God?!'

God spoke back: you need to trust me. I'm God and you're not. Let's remember that you can't see the future but I can, I made the world and run it, not you' (most of chapters 38 through 41)

God taught Job that he was never abandoned. Though, by earthly standards, things were really bad God didn't leave and He does care and He does have a plan.

Job learned not to just "revere" God outwardly; Job acquired heart knowledge. He learned to rely on God no matter what the situation (chapter 42).

There was a really long time that I was similar to Job. I had a tiny bit of head knowledge but no heart knowledge.

I didn't realize that we don't always have to like some*thing* to love some*one*. I compared myself to Job because of the suffering, not because of the learning.

God loved Job so much that He abased him to abound him. God can and does restore. It's that God has a plan that we are part of, not vice versa.

It's that He knows the beginning from the end; He is all powerful; He is so many good things.

Can you be happy in your situation? Not necessarily *because* of your situation but *despite* your situation. If you want to be truly happy, you can't rely on your circumstances to do it.

It's like the rich people that are never satisfied, no matter how much they have. If you're waiting for your life to be as you dream it, it'll always fall short.

Sometimes in the pain of life I still make accusations like Job did. Then I have to remind myself –or actually God is reminding me- who I am and Who He is.

Things get a little rosier then (p.s. read the end of the book of Job).

Chantelle and Danielle arrive with mom. I'm so excited that they're there I forget to thank mom. They help me finish packing up my little bit of clothes, a book and the roses my cousin Renee bought me as a 'get well' gift... I am very unlikely to get well but at least I have nice flowers.

In no time we are out of the hospital. Danielle is pushing me in the wheelchair while Chantelle half walks, half skips alongside. The open spaces and the hard cement parking lot are freaking me right out, but luckily hospitals usually make you leave in a wheelchair.

We three laugh and giggle like nothing has happened. For a moment, I feel really pretty normal.

SO TIGHT- May 18th, 1999

So on the seventeenth; after we drop off Danielle and Chantelle at their houses and go to mine, I get some news: I am going to a group home because I'm a delinquent. Well, not quite a delinquent; Mom and dad want me to be in Saskatoon in case I need to go back to the hospital there. It still feels as bad as delinquency though.

*

I've been here two days, two somewhat interesting days. Going to a group home initially sounded kind of bad but to tell you the truth I was kind of relieved. I feel too broken to face my school mates yet.

I'd like to see my boyfriend, though, but when I phoned him yesterday he showed no indication of planning a trip here any time soon. He just talked about his band and after a few minutes we hung up.

The kids here sort of freak me out. They're all pretty nice –the fact that most of them are boys who want to impress me helps a bit – but they're delinquents. Not the way I called myself one but I was just kidding; *they* really *are* delinquents. They've stolen things or knifed someone or are pyromaniacs or something like that.

The location I'm in, as well as this house, is pretty cool. The workers are pretty interesting and nice too. The other day one lady made hemp and bead necklaces with us. The fact I just mentioned that I like crafts is probably another obvious indication that I am not here due to a crime!

One thing I don't like is my 'curfew'. There's some rule for the delinquents that they can't go out alone until they've gotten enough badges or something. It applies to me too. Not that I see that being a problem. Even if it possibly was, I'm too scared of open spaces –and thugs- to *go* anywhere in order to *do* anything.

There's a lady named Barb who used to go to our church. She has kids and one of them is my age -her name is Sarah Rae. I can go out with if I'm good this week.

They're Christian-y geeks but I just feel like I 'fit' when I'm with them. Sort of like with the teens at my Edam Pentecostal church.

As for my health, I have had one seizure here so far and just a petit mal. I don't even know what medication I'm on but maybe it's stopping me from falling unconscious and convulsing, so I guess that's something.

But while going out for a few hours might be fun, I can't forget 'where' I am. I don't mean 'where' as in location- I mean state of mind and body and all that. Even though I have new medication, the fear has not lessened at all.

The fear and anxiety seems worse than the seizures… although the time I peed my pants during a grand mal makes this theory a little questionable.

Yesterday, when I was just walking down the hallway in the house, I became crazy terrified. Where the hallway ends and the kitchen begins, there is a little table.

Well, I ran down the hallway and basically flung myself at the table but missed and banged my face on the leg of the chair. Now my lips are all bruised up and I look like such a moron.

There's *no* chance that I'm telling people –including my parents-how it all happened.

*

The juvenile delinquents and I get in the group home van, driven by one of the group home workers. After a half hour's drive, we get to some delinquent school that I could never find myself, there are so many twists and turns.

It's not just my delinquent youth home 'family' that attend this school (which actually is a small office building or something). There are other kids who I guess are other delinquents from other group homes.

I'm one of the only kids that are even *in* a grade, or at least don't take modified classes or something. There's one kid that's older than me, but he's in grade eight.

I find them and this set-up kind of ridiculous but it's also kind of fun and okay. At least no one is making fun of me for seizures and a phobia that I swear I can't make go away as much as I will myself to calm and be normal.

One day I hung on to a worker for 5 minutes, crying. We were all going to go for a walk and I was terrified. No one poked fun (at least to my face). That would never be the case in Edam.

IRIDESCENT

You see my smile
But my heart cries;
It's been awhile
With this disguise.
My smile is there
And Just for you
But I despair,
What should I do?
I want to tell you what I feel,
I want you to understand.
My happiness you see isn't real,
This disguise needs to come to an end.
The me you don't see is my frown,
And you don't see my tears,
But I just cannot come around
To tell you all my fears,
I am really a roaring bear
But I am in a tiny shell.
I am a flower o-so-rare,
And I am living in this hell.

But I can't tell you the truth,
You're happier not knowing at all,
Yet I would tell you if you choose
To listen when I call

MEETING THE BEATLES IN WIDE OPEN SPACES - June 10th, 1999

It's June 10th, 1999. I've been here for nearly a month. I've learned to like it here and then hate it and then like it and now I can't do it anymore. One of the reasons is because I discovered that I'm 'horrible' but for no reason I've experienced before.

At first I thought the people here would never judge me badly. No one said anything negative when I was scared or seized so I thought we were golden.

But it turns out that I'm such a freak that even when I'm not a delinquent, I still don't fit in. They make fun of me because I'm too 'good' and 'nice' and 'safe.'

If I'm not an outcast for what I *have*, I am an outcast for who I *am*. There is no reason for me to stay here with crappy school and without my family or friends.

*

So I phone my house and mom answers. She can tell I have something important to talk about, but I ask for dad. When he gets on the line I scream that I want them to come get me right now. I tell him about the goody two shoes thing and that I don't have any reason to be here.

About doing school work at the weird delinquent school where there are no actual classrooms or deadlines or structure. That if I accidentally offend someone here, they might steal something or hurt me. That I am *not* better but I probably will not need to be rushed to the RUH. There are no reasons not to come home.

"It is 9:00 P.M. Blaire," dad says, "We can't come get you right now but we'll come in the morning." I am crying.

He says, "Don't worry Blue-air"- my favorite nickname, he knows just what to say because in spite of myself a smile tickles the corners of my mouth- "you have not done anything wrong."

Then he points out that it's too late in the year to begin grade ten, but he's pretty sure that getting the teacher to send homework with Fabian will be fine. Next school year I'll start grade eleven with my class though.

Sounds just fine to me.

LARGELY GONE

The wind blows lightly on my face,
Showing me my disgrace,
Mocking all the things that I truly miss, like the warmth on my feet
from the
grass' soft kiss;
And walking on the beach out in the sand
Is what I now fear in this large open land;
But who hears me when at night I cry
Of happy days spent, long gone by?
Not fearing that which is so gentle and free
Are the memories that are all lost to me.
Finding happiness in a large open field,
Standing amidst the farmer's new yield,
Are the dreams I dream day by day
As those dreams blow me farther away
From long ago joys that I once knew
To this small space, abandoned
By You

GRADE 11: A DIFFERENT KIND OF BLAH- OCTOBER 8TH 1999

I've been in grade eleven for over a month now. Besides the few grand mal seizures I had in May, my life is no different than the past three years of hell.

The phobia of open spaces still makes no sense to me- I mean, why do I get so lucky as to have two wacko things wrong with me? I am terrified of every space, everywhere.

I still feel like I might fly apart every time I stand up. I still jump from desk to desk when no one is looking and cling to walls and door handles for comfort.

I tell people that I'm fine when I'm *so* not. I try to rely on myself although it's obviously not working. Sometimes my blood pressure rises and my heart beats so fast that I have a seizure. Or just about go insane anyway.

One might think that I'd be depressed, but not so. Sadness hits me often, but depression not so much. I basically feel numb; I'm sort of hopeless but I feel so void of feeling that I don't care to hope in the first place. I just don't want to think or do or be.

I rarely stay home from school now; I'm not exactly sure why. I still look ridiculous when others see me have seizures and fall down. My classmates were told that I have seizures but they still think that the anxiety I say I feel is just made up and that I am at fault for pretty much everything.

It hurts that they think I'm a 'weirdo liar' who deserves only crappy things. When they found out in grade ten that I was on the honor roll I heard all about the injustice of it from all but a handful of people –mostly the boys actually. **But also Danielle and Chantelle even though they are supposed to be my best friends.**

THE END...

No one needed. You. Ever.

But once. One time.

A long time. Ago.

Someone. Was.

It was great. So great.

Everyone said. So.

You Just smiled.

They were right.

You knew.

You were high. On you.

If it went away

You laugh.

But you were wrong.

And you cried. And you cried.

Time went by.

Slowly.

All. Alone.

Why?

Do you. Understand?

And you missed.

So much. So very.

Not needed. Anymore.

Anymore.

And you cried.

So bad. You were so.

Bad.

It was good. Good.

For a while.

But no.

And you cried. And cried.

And they did. Cried.

Why? Why.

Because You had never?

Weren't needed?

WOULD YOU LIKE A LITTLE HOPE WITH YOUR FRIES?- OCTOBER 9TH 1999, 9:33 P.M.

So I'm sitting on my bedroom floor, looking at nothing really and reflecting on the sad life that I am merely *surviving*. The doctors don't think I'll ever have a real job, family or anything good. And if that's what they say, as maddening as they are, is there anything else to believe in or hope for?

There's a knock on my bedroom door. With little inflection I say, "Come in," and Mom enters looking pretty excited; Dad follows. Why are they both happy and better yet, why are they even *here*?

I definitely don't want to get up off the floor because moping is best done if I sit in a pose of uninterrupted abject despair. "So how are you feeling today Blaire?" This is a very stupid question and I'm very suspicious. Sarcastically I answer, "Oh I'm just planning the next rager that I'm throwing since I'm all better and everything."

Dad chuckles and I become mad because I don't think there's anything funny at all. What's hilarious about being hopeless and in constant mental agony (and that's not even including when I seize for no apparent reason)?

Not paying any attention to my grimace, he grabs my hands and pulls me up off the floor. Now I'm really mad and very hurt too: he's the last person on earth I'd expect to not be sensitive of my depressed, scared and fragile feelings and he's acting all gay and merry.

Before I can say anything smart, though, dad looks at mom and says, "You tell her," in a conspiratorial way. "Tell me *what?*" I ask in a way that says, 'hurry up so you can get out of my room and I can get back to my important job of doing nothing and hating everything.'

"We don't want to get you excited about what could be nothing Blaire, but we have some news that could be really good. I have a strong feeling that it could be *really* good." I grimace to show how annoyed and skeptical I am.

She continues as if she never saw my expression: "We looked on the internet the other day. The pills you are on now are little more than a Band-Aid solution. Your dad and I searched the internet for medication that might take care of your kind of seizures and such.

"They call them petit mal but the technical word is partial myo-clonic or something like that." I'm about to say that I really don't care what they're called. Dad cuts in, obviously too excited not to.

Almost vibrating he too-quickly says, "We found a very new-to-Canada type of medication that is available for prescription for seizures. It's called Lamotrigine and after reading the description, we think it sounds like it could be really effective for you."

I begin to say something about Dr. Lory probably not going for it when mom says, "I know you're thinking that we aren't doctors and can't prescribe and of course that's true and so that's an issue.

"That's why a few days ago we contacted Dr. Lory and told him about the Lamotrigine. He started by saying, '...oh well you know, I don't know.'"

Mom looks at me and slyly says, "We told him, 'do it or else, Dr. Lory, because it's not like you have any better ideas... if you have any at all.'"

> Okay, that is not what mom says. And neither does dad. I have no basis whatsoever to say this but I like to think of my parents as heroes that sweep in and save me from a lifetime of seizures while the doctors sit back, dumbfounded.
> What mom does say is that, "He prescribed some for you and we have the pills here, we picked them up from the pharmacy yesterday."

Mom pulls out something from behind her back. Closer inspection shows me that it's a pill bottle. I get up from my bed –where I had ended up after dad lifted me off the floor.For the first time since leaving RUH several months ago, I am a little bit interested in something.

Trying to be unbelievably non-chalant and disinterested-sounding and looking, I aside, "So I am supposed to take these, like, right now?" "Yeppers," says dad.

He continues, "The pharmacist at Shop-rite told me that the doctor has indicated that you start on a pretty small dose and then you can go up from there. I'll get you the next, higher dose in two weeks' time."

"Well," I begin to say, "I guess it can't get any worse, right?" **Though I've been burned before by a million medications that hardly or never worked, I am more hopeful than I've been for a while.**

777- *November 10th, 1999*

I pay little attention to this nice, early November day, as preoccupied as I am with spinning. I feel like I'm living inside a VLT or slot machine.

I whine to Danielle, "I swear that I'll never be able to eat again!" I say with a painful whine in my voice. She just shoots at me, "Stop being so dramatic and immature, it's not that bad Blaire!"

I continue to whine, "I am so freakin' dizzy! I can't even stand up straight." Then I say in even more of a whine, "Not that you'd know, the world isn't spinning uncontrollably for you."

We're on our way up the stairs to the Home Ec. lab; Danielle is holding my arm and half dragging me. All the while she clenches her teeth and speaks in a mean stage whisper (mean like cruel, not awesome).

This has been my deal for several weeks. I have no idea what is wrong and neither does anyone else. I am plagued with the inability to see or stand straight and sometimes both at the same time. I feel nauseous, tired and grumpy and I don't care about anything but not because I'm sad and hopeless, because of… I don't know what.

I haven't worn make-up to school for weeks and haven't done my hair for about that long either. Mom and dad let me sleep in till about fifteen minutes before the bus most days since I am so tired.

***

A little over a week later, I'm in the church basement with my friend Heidi. I have double vision with intermittent 'VLT sight', meaning that the images in my eyes spin like video lottery terminal fruit and number sevens.

Heidi and I are talking about something while heading to the door to go upstairs when suddenly my face bangs up against something really hard. It kind of feels like carpet but I can't see to be sure. Inappropriately, I laugh.

Heidi bends over and frantically asks if I'm okay. It's only now that I can see a little; I am definitely on the floor with my face smooshed into the brown-burgundy carpet.

I kind of laugh and say that I am fine- I'm not hurt except for a little bit of rug burn on my chin. I didn't fall out of phobic fear. I actually haven't felt much fear at all in the past week or two.

I don't have much control over my bodily movements, but I am not embarrassed or uncomfortable like I am when I lose control and seize.

Heidi looks at me like we really should do something and inquires in a tone fully of worry, "Should we tell someone?" "No, it's fine," I reply nonchalantly and wave it off with my hand –although I can't see exactly which direction she is so I may have waved at the wall behind me.

Heidi might not be familiar with drunks but I know all too well that this is what one looks like and I stifle another laugh.

*

I am in no way worried about my moment in the basement. On the way home, though, I do think about it. I had no idea I was even falling till I hit carpet.

'Why,' I contemplate, 'was that?' I conclude that I have very little depth perception, and at some points it lessens even more dramatically.

I suppose that some people know that this is obviously so, but I just became aware of this and I feel smart. And vaguely interested.

GROSSMUTTER
VERSUS PETRA –
November 16th, 1999

I'm at my Gramma McCaffrey's house. I feel nauseous crappy, which in no way surprises me.

I suddenly remember something that I briefly noted to myself a few days ago, but then had quickly forgotten: I am not very scared- not even though I am standing in the middle of Gramma's dining room right now. I haven't even had a seizure for over a week, or so I surmise.

Gramma is near the china cabinet, where I usually would be because it is something I can grab onto. I think, 'maybe she has a phobia too' and giggle to myself.

I am staring at her, although I am not sure which of the two images of her that I currently see is actually her. What I do notice is her dark brown (never dyed), short permed hair and think that she looks a little old and uncool but hey, don't most grandmas?

I then realize that noticing her hair is uncharacteristic of me- I don't usually notice *much* about others. When you are encompassed by fear, it is hard to exert much energy in noticing things. That sounds very selfish, I know, but being terrified all day, every day doesn't leave you a lot of time or ability to think of anything else. And for some reason my memory is incredibly short (like, you can be my best friend but if I don't or rarely see you for a year, good luck hoping that I'll miss you).

Gramma is looking at something in the wood and glass china cabinet against the wall. Without turning to look at me, Gramma, says, "So den you 'aven't had any fits in quite a long time then, 'ey?" You have got to love her terminology.

"No, I guess not," I begin to respond, "but I haven't had much time to think about it." I think, 'she just stole my thoughts right out of my head. I hope she didn't also hear my thoughts about her hair.'

Out loud I say, "Maybe I'm just having a good week or two. I mean, that doesn't happen too often but I'm kind of dizzy and probably in more way than one."

"So has your head straightened out that fear too?"-I hate it when people mention something like my fear being all in my head but I don't address it. "I wouldn't say that it's gone, but I am not too scared right now."(side note: there's a big difference between noticing that something should be bothering you -like I still have many times in the past few weeks- versus actually being terrified that you are going to die of fear).

I say, "I think everything took a break because God thought that it was too, like, cruel for me to have this dizziness and have to deal with being terrified of open spaces and have seizures too."

"Okay. Now go and get the Christmas lights upstairs, the blue ones in the left crawl space." I like that, like Brandon when I had a seizure on stage and he acted like nothing happened, she doesn't get all serious on me too often. I whistle happily all the way upstairs, holding on to the wall the whole way.

I bump the walls a few times, not able to gauge how close they are to me, but I am happy.

PUKING PUDDLES –November 17th, 1999

One day after my 'happy' day with Gramma, I wake up again feeling like a grouchy crap ball. I go to the kitchen thinking that for some reason eating might make me feel a little better... as it often does.

Mom and dad are in the kitchen and I sit down. I ask mom to pour me a bowl of cereal and she does. I think it's Shreddies © but I'm not sure because I can't really see. I am not very hungry, but like I said, maybe eating will help.

It's a weekend and I'm not sure where Fabian and Nikki are, but then I stop thinking about it. I don't have the ambition to care today.

Mom brings me the cereal and pulls out a chair for me. I am talking to dad and eating a few bites of my cereal at the same time. Slowly my words start to stretch out.

I suddenly can see even less than I do in this 'new normal.' It feels kind of like I'm hearing through a puddle and I'm also trying to think while I'm being drowned by it.

Then I can't even lift my finger.My fingers, I am sure, are huge and won't fit around my spoon. I am not sure if anyone else heard this comment, though, because I don't know if I am actually able to speak.

Fingers huge or not, they don't work properly and I am not able to hold it. It falls to the floor in dramatic slow motion- I can't really see this, but I imagine its slow descent. With a weird, dulled sound I hear it hit the table and bounce off onto the floor, leaving a puddle of milk behind.

I reflect that mom will be mad. I want to giggle but I can't. As I expected, greatly annoyed, mom says, "What are you doing Blaire?!" I can't see her, though, because she is off to my side somewhere. I'm unable to turn my head but even if I could, my eyes are too blurry to see and to finish off, my head flops sideways and won't right itself.

"Blaire, your mom is speaking to you!" dad says irately. I want to say something, I really do, but I can't. My mouth kind of hangs open because I can't stop it. Milk dribbles down my chin. He continues, "Blaire, why won't you eat your cereal?"

I say nothing (obviously) so after a brief moment he repeats himself: "Blaire, answer!" "We have to take her in to emergency at the Lady Minto again," mom says but actually meaning that *dad* will take me, "But first let's see if we can get her to eat a bit more."

I hate being talked about when I'm right there but what else would anyone do in this sci-fi type of moment? Mom then tries to feed me cereal and fails. She throws her hands up and brushes the back of her head and neck with them in frustration: "Well, this isn't working so off you two go." She gives dad an 'I love you'.

He tries to get me to walk to the truck but ends up just kind of dragging me. He opens the door for me and then, annoyed that I won't cooperate, demands, "Put on your seatbelt!"I do no such thing so he lifts me up and puts me on the seat and my head lolls to the side.

I think to myself, 'This is hilarious!' but obviously he doesn't share the sentiment. He yells, "What the he#& is wrong with you?"

I think that he might be yelling because he's scared. I also note that he doesn't do up my seat-belt for me and oddly and sarcastically laugh inside.

Once we arrive at the hospital I can move even less than before if that's even possible- dad has to outright carry me in. The first person we see -well, I only hear him because I am kind of facing sideways- is Dr. Dewitt. He checks my vitals.

He then tells the nurse, "Get me a syringe." I wonder what on earth he can give me at this juncture in my life. I mean, what is good for 'frozen body syndrome'?

As I am wondering, the nurse walks back into the room with a syringe containing some sort of liquid but since I have no peripheral.... "I've got the Valium ©," says the nurse who I can't see.

It seems odd to me that they are giving me the same thing that they gave me several months earlier. You know, the time they gave it to slow my seizures.

Only moments later, I feel someone sticking a needle into my right hip. And the wonderful feeling of cool liquid going into my body (note: I am not a drug addict though it may seem that way).

Soon I can move again. I talk very quickly to dad. I realize that I make little sense, but at the same time, I think my words are very deep and intelligent.

***

Six days later I'm in the living room on our couch. Mom, dad and Nikki are going somewhere. I don't feel like going for two reasons. One: I have no ambition and two, I can't see straight- looking straight at strangers who then have to tell me that what I think is their face is really the bathroom sign doesn't interest me.

Less than twenty minutes later they're gone and I am still in the living room. That's when I feel the 'frozen' coming on. Not sure how to explain the feeling that indicates what is happening, but I know.

My swirly vision starts to become puddle-ish. I speak some words out loud just to hear if my voice is slow too: it is. I know that I am about to be paralyzed and though I don't understand it at all, I know what to do.

Fabian is downstairs but there's no way I'd call him for help. My throat could be swelling in anaphylactic shock and I don't think I would call him.

For a second I think about how mean he is and then I think that what I am currently thinking is extra stupid since my body is busy going numb.

And even if I *wanted* his help, I am less able by the second to speak or move. If I tried to get to him, I'd probably fall down the stairs. 'The best bet at this moment', I think, 'is to lay on the couch and go to sleep.'

So I close my eyes, my right arm hanging limply off of the couch. What if my paralysis won't go away by itself? Maybe when mom and dad get back they'll find me frozen- or worse yet, dead.

I start thinking of witty puns that would fit this moment- I am so weird. How about, 'I sure like moments frozen in time... or at least paralyzed.

Then everything goes black and that is all I know.

YOU HAVE TO DRAW A LINE SOMEWHERE –December 9th, 1999

It's December 9th and I'm sitting in my desk in the grade eleven homeroom, seeing straight. I can't believe it, another day where everything is fine. There's hardly any fear, there are no seizures and the dizziness and nausea are completely gone.

One of the sucky readers is reading out loud right now. Mr. Merkosky is standing there in between the aisles of students. I want this kid to be done the paragraph that Mr. Merk gave them and just move on to another reader who is hopefully much better.

All of a sudden Mr. Merkosky says, in a tone that suggests he's repeating himself, "Blaire, please start reading." I love reading anything in general but, I think, especially reading out loud in a group. I rarely falter on a word, have a great narrative voice and I can pronounce almost anything; I love appearing great at something, even if it is something like this.

I look at the page and that's when I realize I have a little problem: the words on the page are swimming. I can make out individual words but it's when taken collectively, they just float in the air.

I want to comment to Mr. Merk- though something stops me-that the book has gone crazy. I'm sure the words that were printed are all just gibberish because no two seem to make for the beginning of a normal sentence.

I am not sure what to do so I hesitate. I can feel eyes on me and I'm kind of embarrassed but kind of not. One thing I've become very accustomed to over the years is having the spotlight –whether good or bad- on me.

Better yet, I've realized that a lot of things that people find embarrassing are *not* embarrassing; I've had the pleasure of knowing the feeling of people thinking you're broken and need help or else that you're just plain lying and want you to shut up.

I think to put the ruler underneath every line on the page; I dig in my pencil case until I locate it. I put it under the first line in the paragraph that I am about to read and voila, I can see just fine.

Oh, just another day in the life of Blaire LaClare!

IT'S JUST NOT RITE
–January 2000

We are sitting at the table: me, mom and dad. It seems that almost every important thing in some way revolves around the kitchen and/or kitchen table. It is a Saturday and I eat my cereal, mom moves around the kitchen, dad sits next to me and my siblings are somewhere that I don't think much about.

I am wearing my hair in clips which seems insignificant, but it's not for me at this point in time. Almost the whole time that I was 'dizzy' I only wore my hair in a haphazard pony or messy and down. The first time since then –last week- that I wore clips in it, Danielle told me how not sloppy I looked finally.

I've also actually not snapped at people for a couple days too. For the past three months, I've snapped at pretty much everyone at school. Even at Stephanie while we baked in Home. Ec., although I knew how bad that was as soon as the words left my mouth. Stephanie is the nicest person in the world; even when I couldn't see straight, I knew I'd crossed a line.

It's past 10 A.M. and I haven't taken my pills yet so I grab my bottle of pills (the lamotrigine/Lamictal) and take it to the table with me. I need something to wash them down and instead of getting water, I'll take the pills to my bowl and just drink some milk.

I swallow my pills and set down the bottle on the table next to where dad is, by chance, sitting. He looks at the pills and then he looks away. He pauses for a few seconds and then he looks back.

He now is standing up with my pill bottle in hand, going toward the pill cupboard. He says, "Hey Blaire, do you still have the pill bottle from your first prescription of Lamictal?"

"Yeah..." I say nonchalantly but hesitantly. I wonder what he could possibly be getting at. I am terrified by the idea that this might be a repeat of wanting to take my pills away from me, like that time before I went to the Edam hospital, so what is happening?

He carries both the old, empty bottle and the full, new bottle to the table. He reads the label on the old one, "100 mg." Then he picks up the new one and looks at the pills. He says, "50 milligrams, hmmm" and it's obvious he's considering something. But what?

Finally he says kind of in a concerned voice, "Oh wow." He leans back in his chair, puts his hands over his head and it's not until the chair lands back on the floor that he says, "Oh I get it, I really get it."

"What on earth do you get dad?" I ask, lost. He indicates to the bottle, "Look Blaire, the old bottle says *more* milligrams than the new pills do. That means that you were getting a higher dosage however many weeks ago"- I cut in because now I get it-

"So that's why I was so dizzy. That's why I couldn't see or think. Oh my gawd dad, this is insane!" I shoot while grasping and squeezing both temples with each respective hand.

*

It's another Saturday. Everything is the same except that dad is missing. And it's not morning, it's late afternoon. Dad isn't, of course, 'missing, missing.' He's gone to North Battleford.

This morning he told me that when he returns this afternoon he'll have something to talk with me about. When he said this I was a little worried, which he ascertained, and he reassured me that I was not in trouble.

So I'm sitting at the table, not really doing anything. Me and mom are talking a bit but mostly she's preoccupied with reorganizing the cupboard and I'm preoccupied with lazy thoughts of not much of anything.

I hear the crunch of gravel and then the pull of tires onto a cement pad and I know that dad is home in the cherry red dodge. Mom stops arranging and says, a little redundantly because we obviously both know this, "Oh, your dad is home."

A few seconds after I hear the dodge being shut off, dad opens the porch door and walks in. I hear immediately, "Greetings and salutations" and I giggle a little. Dad is so quirky and awesome.

Dad says, "Oh hello Elaine, how was your day?" and plants a kiss on her lips before continuing, "Oh kidlets, I'm home!" I gesture at him to make him aware of my presence. I say, "but I don't know where Fabian and Nikki, downstairs maybe," and out of the corner of my eye I see mom smirk and thumb towards the door to indicate they're actually outside.

"So what do you have to talk to me about?" I excitedly yip at dad. "Hold on Blaire, I haven't even had a chance to sit down," he says.

After he's in the chair with a (fairly) fresh brownie and some coffee in front of him, he says almost as an aside, "So one of the places I went today was to Shop-Rite Drugs," he says.

I wonder to myself why he would say something so boring in answer to his teen's question. As if I really care if he went, like, to the drug store. Then the reason sort of dawns on me and I say/ask, "Oh, where you got my prescription filled the first time I got it, and then just a few weeks ago?"

"Yeah. Well the thing is that I noticed that your dizziness stopped immediately after you were done your first bottle of pills. So I looked at the nearly empty first bottle. It said *more* milligrams than you are currently on. You were taking a double dose.

I'm immediately turn from happy to enraged and shout, "Who could do such a thing to me?! I can't believe this happened! That pharmacist almost killed me! I couldn't see anything but double or spinning for nearly three months!

"I didn't care that I looked like a total mess for nearly three months. I couldn't stay awake or be nice to people! My grades suffered because I was so spacy and lost! This is not, like, cool at all! I almost died when my body got paralyzed man!"

I look over and mom has her hand on her chin with one finger up over her mouth. She is shaking her head in disbelief and finally says, "Well what did you do then Paul?" He replies, "I went into Shop-Rite and told them that one of the pharmacists on staff had given my daughter a double dose of pills and she had become very sick.

"I don't imagine anyone will be losing their job- which wasn't what I was trying to do anyway. But I told them in no uncertain terms that I would be taking my business elsewhere."

"That's it dad? Your daughter almost kicks the bucket from someone's stupid screw up and all you can say is that you will take your, like, business elsewhere?!"

I'm justifiably beyond revved up. Dad doesn't reply because, honestly, what kind of reply is good?

LAMICTDON- February 27th, 2000

It's nearly 2 months later; my fear hasn't really come back; it rears its ugly head for a few seconds sometimes and I feel like flying apart, but nothing happens- the seizures are gone.

I kind of think that maybe the fact I was on that double dose of Lamictal © was kind of good. It was mostly horrible, don't get me wrong, but it might have been a bit of a blessing in disguise.

I mean, with so much medication in my system, besides not being able to see straight and not being able to move or talk twice, my seizures might have had no other choice than to just quit.

I never had much time to think about seizures or fear in that first three months on Lamictal©. I think that my healing from the meds was actually fast-forwarded... if that makes sense. I've never shared this cock-a-brained theory of mine with anyone else and probably never will, but I think about it.

> God does not cause evil in our lives. The Bible says that He is the giver of all good gifts
> (James 1:17) which is true, everything he gives us is good.

But sometimes God lets things that look 'bad' to us happen because they are in some way beneficial in the long run.

It is not pointless suffering, the Bible is clear on that.

1 Peter 6-7 says, "...[we] greatly rejoice, even though now for a little while, if necessary, [we] have been distressed by various trials, so that the proof of [our] faith... may be found to result in praise and glory and honor at the revelation of Jesus Christ" (1 Peter 1:6-7).

In Lamentations chapter three, the prophet Jeremiah is *lamenting* the "grief" that God "causes" (v. 32a) but also acknowledges His "abundant lovingkindness." (v. 32b). Furthermore, he rhetorically asks, "Is it not from the mouth of the Most High that both good and ill go forth?" (Lam. 3:38).

Don't think that you have to understand all of the things He does, because He is not us and we are not Him... have you created the world today? Or orchestrated someone's life so everything that is supposed to happen, happens *when* it happens and for a reason?

Have you died on a cross, been buried in a tomb and rose again?

There's just one thing that we absolutely have to know: God loves us unfathomably (ex: Jeremiah 29:11, 1 John 4:9-11, Isaiah 54:10, Romans 8:37-9,

Romans 5:8, 2 Samuel 22:1-8, Isaiah 54:4-11, Ephesians 2:4-5, Psalm 86:15, John 15:13, Deuteronomy 7:9, Philippians 4:6-7, Psalm 37:9,

Micah 7:7-8, Psalm 139:13-16, Job 3:16, 2 Peter 3:9, Psalm 23:1-6, Psalm 44:3, Psalm 55:22, Psalm 62:7, Psalm 73:26, Psalm 84:11, Psalm 91:3-7, Micah 6:3, John 3:16, John 8:7-10, and on and on and on...)

SURROUNDED AND ALONE

I sit in this chair alone.

People everywhere.

They don't see my on my own.

And they really don't care.

"Just one of the girls", is what I say,

But I don't mean it, they make me sick.

They laugh, they giggle, they carry on that way,

They gather in their group, their "click".

Do they see the despair in my eyes?

Am I all alone?

Do they notice my heart's demise,

Will they make me face this on my own?

A TALL DRINK OF WATER JULY 1ST 2000

A few months back- just a few months before grade eleven was over- I went to a dance in the weird little town of Glaslyn. It's right next to Edam but for being so close, I barely knew it even was there.

There was a guy at the dance named John Koop (pronounced Cope, not Coop!), the best friend of Danielle's Glaslyn boyfriend. I danced with John all evening; it was kind of like a dream.

He's totally tall with dark skin... and he's hot. I was extremely taken with him and him with me by the looks of it. He liked that I am so fragile –the RUH thing last year took a lot out of me- kind of like an 'I want to take care of you' thing.

It's weird, though, because even though I liked him then, I never paid any attention to him after the dance. I have just finally gotten my seizures under control so I can't think of much else, even guys. This is something Danielle and my other close friends and my parents would totally guffaw at.

Then a few months later John and I met up again and John asked if Danielle and I wanted to go driving and partying for July 1st so here we are.

YIPPEE YAHOO

Today is graduation and here I am, breaking expectations. No one really expected me to graduate like a normal person. Almost *definitely,* no one expected me to graduate with a gorgeous man by my side, but I am.

John is super patient and awesome; I told him that he's probably the nicest guy I've ever met in my whole life. I think that my parents actually like him better than me. That's okay though because I could see how anyone would fall in love with him.

Being with John helps the occasional anxiety I still feel. It's mostly gone but it still comes on sometimes, always without warning. I wonder if it's just a habit of being terrified of open spaces for years something.

Of course John doesn't know that I have anxiety or that he's helping me. He holds my hand and stands near me almost all the time without even knowing I need him to. Anyway, the fear of open spaces dwindles a bit all the time.

This is the first time in a long time that I've felt normal -well, just about. A few months ago, -so a pretty long time- John and I were driving on the road to Picnic Lake.

Just sitting in the truck, I suddenly became terrified of how big the space seemed. I was also scared that I was going to have a 'lose control' (when I say 'lose control' it's kind of a feeling like I'm being ripped in a million directions and might explode and die).

I know to the average person it sounds like I have agoraphobia, but I don't. It's not that I get scared of being around too many people in case something happens.

I'm actually scared of the space itself, and not wanting to lose my mind in front of others just reasonably is to be expected. I guess you might only get that nuance if you've had anxiety and especially if you have seizures as well.

***

It's Christmas break in 2003- I'm in my 3rd year of university. This Christmas is extra exciting because on December 27th John and I are getting married! Not to detract from that, I'm also five months pregnant!

***

Avery Gilbert is born on June 2nd, 2004. Gilbert was my grandpa LaClare's name -he died before I was born. But we really gave him that middle name because Gilbert is the name of one of my favorite cousins- my double first cousin to be exact.

Avery is 10 pounds, 8 ounces. I can't even believe it. I guess that's what I should have expected, since I ate chocolate for nearly 9 months straight, I gained a zillion pounds and retained water like I was a fish in the sea.

He was not planned, yet he totally was. The night before I found out that I was pregnant with him, I dreamt that I was shopping for blue baby clothes.I knew when I woke up that morning that I was pregnant.

And I was much more excited and happy than not. I was apprehensive to have to tell my parents that their unmarried university daughter was pregnant but I was thrilled.

I wanted Avery without ever knowing that I wanted Avery. He is one of the very best things that has ever happened to me. **He is my beautiful boy and I adore him.**

14 - MARCH 2TH, 2005

At the Glaslyn Fall Supper tonight our 9 month old starts screaming and won't stop. We tell Adam, Denis and Nathan that we won't be coming to our weekly game of poker.

We haven't even gotten our shoes off and the phone rings; John answers it. He talks for a minute and kind of sounds 'funny'.

When he gets off the phone I ask who it was and what they wanted. He just tells me to sit down and I know this is serious. I tell him that I don't want to sit down and he asks again. I moan, "Did something happen to grandma LaClare?!" and he says no.

I think that if nothing has happened to her, then there can be no real problem; I let out a sigh of relief. Then John takes my breath away as he says,

"Your dad just died of a massive heart attack."

I can't even compute what I am hearing. He is only 47 years old and he is in good shape. Heck, today he even went snowboarding (like he often does).

I mean, yeah, he's had heart burn for the past week or so but still....

John tells me that that was my mom on the phone. I don't know if I'm crying right now because I am in a world that doesn't feel real; my surroundings, my body, my grouchy baby all don't feel real.

Now John's mom and dad are in our little porch. I wonder how they can possibly know already. Carol and Henry hug me and I hug them like the world will float away if I don't hang on for dear life.

Carol says, "I will help you pack. What do you need me to pack?" I can't respond because I can't think. Except that I suddenly say, "Where is Avery? I have to take care of Avery." I suddenly understand how mom could phone us, even in the face of such tragedy.

*

We are near mom's and dad's place where we're going. Because of course that's what you do when someone dies. I have stopped crying and don't know how to feel. A thought –a great, happy thought, suddenly comes to mind.

I ask, "John, what did mom exactly say when she phoned you? Exactly, word for word. "Did she say that dad died?" He replies hesitantly, "She said that your dad was gone." He has no idea what I'm asking.

"Oh!" I say, relieved. "One time, when dad's friend Roy was in the hospital, dad asked his other friend how Roy was. Darren said that Roy hadn't made it out of the hospital so dad assumed the obvious. He found out the next day what Darren really meant which was that he was just still in the hospital."

I kind of giggle awkwardly and say, "So mom was probably just saying the same thing and it's okay. Dad is probably just in the hospital, that's all. He's probably going to be fine!"

I now feel almost exuberant. John is looking at me like he does not really think that that is true. He says nothing to break my new-found relief but I can tell he just thinks I'm in denial. Finally he says, "Maybe," but he doesn't sound convincing at all.

Then we are in mom's and dad's yard. There are a lot of vehicles there. My hope deflates. I run to the house and the second the door is open (I don't know who opens it), I collapse.

I think that I collapse into Nikki's and mom's arms but I'm not sure, I can't really focus on things.Auntie Cami and Uncle Denis, Suzanne's and Amy's parents, are the next people I see. Uncle Denis is the one, I think, that pulls me up on the floor. And then somehow I'm on the couch with my head on his shoulder. I am crying and crying and crying.

Even though I just saw them (well, sort of), I now don't know where Nikki and mom are. I hear the voices of a lot of people but I don't know who they are. I look around and John is holding Avery. I can't tell if John is crying because I can't see his face.

I know that Avery is not making a noise, though. It seems like his crying has served its purpose for the night and now he is done. Some time goes by... it is really dark- it's like a moment frozen in time... or something dramatic.

*

It's a couple of hours later. Several of us are now sitting at the table and things are a little calmer. The outside door opens and Auntie Moni (Mo-NEE) and Auntie Patti (Pu-TEE) come into the house. I get up and I hug them. In this horrible yet happy way, I am enjoying this. I love having our entire –well, almost- extended family together in one place.

Shortly after this, Suzanne comes through the same door. She drove the two and half hours from Saskatoon and though it is late, she is here. I go to her and hug her, now aware of the people around.

***

I am standing in the main aisle in Walmart. We are there to get some nice little shoes for Avery to wear to the funeral. The baby boy clothes are several aisles over so I am not sure why we are where we are... maybe we need conditioner?

We just got here from Bootlegger in the Territorial mall. Trying on clothes there, I was actually, truly a little bit happy. Nikki said she doesn't care what she wears and just grabbed something.

Some lady that I vaguely know comes toward us. She asks friendly but seriously, "how are you doing?" I look at her, unsure how to answer because I think it's kind of a weird question...and also because I suddenly feel like Nikki did in Bootlegger.

Blankly I say, "My dad is dead." I am not angry at her, I do not think she's insensitive, I do not think anything at this moment in time- I just have a feeling of heaviness.

"I know," she says compassionately, and then I don't see her anymore- not because she isn't there but I am having my first real panic attack.

I can no longer really see the people milling around me. Everything is kind of floating around me or, a better explanation would be, spinning hectically. I know where I am but I can't really think about it.

"Blaire," John calls me and then again I hear, "Blaire, are you okay?" John's arms are on my shoulder or maybe wrapped around me; the spinning is stopping. I think he might be shaking me gently to try to bring me back from wherever I was. I say, "Yeah, it's fine; I'm fine," but I don't know if that's true.

Nikki has wandered down a side aisle. Suddenly she is back. Suddenly we are walking to the truck because we have paid for whatever it is that we got.

***

It's been a few months since he died. In all of this, I have started talking to Auntie Cami on the phone a lot. She and Uncle are kind of taking us under their wings.

I say, "Nikki is so sad, even more than me I think but I don't mean that in a bad way, as if I don't miss him immensely too. "But it's different for Nikki- she *experienced* him; she lived with him so he was there every single day.

"I have John and I have Avery to help me. Nikki has mom but it's not like with John because he wasn't his kid or spouse. So I don't grieve for an experience, I grieve for memories.

"She grieves for everything. I mean, of course I don't just remember him distantly like as if I didn't spend a lot of time with him, even though I'm a wife and mother, but it's different."

"That's pretty insightful," Auntie Cami says and though she's probably just trying to be nice, I appreciate it.

I have another person to support me: Suzanne. She phones me quite a bit and listens when I tell her stuff like that I've been lying on the floor that morning, slobbering and wailing because I miss him so much.

LIFE UNINTERRUPTED

Our second son, Austin, came along in 2006. He is so beautiful it's not even funny. I am in love with him; he is the perfect addition to our family.

He is 7 pounds even, which is pretty big since the doctors think he's 4-6 weeks early! His middle name is John- no explanation needed.

Being pregnant with him wasn't super easy. I developed this creepy crawly thing that my new neurologist calls Restless Leg Syndrome.

One weekend, when I was pregnant, we went to John's cousin's wedding. On the way back, it was like my legs were floating (a little like when I was admitted to the Edam hospital but a little different).

Still, with neither of my pregnancies did I have seizures or fear or anything close to it. And now, with Austin a few months old, I'm actually finding that the Lamictal© is feeling toxic. The doctor told me that I could take a little less- seeing double is not a good thing!

WHY

Why do I feel that everything
i do
is nothing?
why do I go everywhere
and arrive
Nowhere?
why do I sense it all
but you
Are still gone

WITH A BANG BANG HERE AND A BANG BANG THERE

John farms, leaving early in the morning (usually around six) and coming home late. He works hard on the farm all day and then often skins coyotes and beavers for hours in the evening.

It's awesome that he's not lazy and he has ambition, but it sucks a lot too. I didn't know when I married him that this is what I was bargaining for. He's tolerant and forgiving and great but the 'never home thing' puts a big kink in life. And, partly because of the lack of time with us, he isn't very connected with the boys or me. It's hard.

And if that all isn't enough, there's hunting season. John loves hunting for himself, but that's not what I mean. He works as a hunting guide for a local outfitter named Carl. He just stays there and we only see him on weekends.

Today is November 14th; we still have more than several weeks to go. I am so extremely lonely almost all of the time and I often cry a lot but today was one of the worst. I broke down at my kitchen table and prayed that God would bring my husband home to me. I phone mom and tell her.

I don't even know why those exact words came out of my mouth.

***

It's 3 days later; the boys and I just left Saulteaux where Avery's hockey team was practicing. Glaslyn's ice isn't artificial so it's not frozen yet. Till ours *is*, we rent, and travel to practices.

Of course I have my bag with my statistics book- I need this course for my Bachelor's in Psychology. My phone is with me too, but it doesn't work half of the time; I need a new one.

It's dark as Avery, Austin and I drive down the highway. Suddenly some truck pulls in front of me and drives down the middle of the road, waving his arms frantically; I look on, dumbfounded.

Finally I realize that the truck belongs to Curt, another one of the hockey parents... who also seems like *my* parent. He pulls over on the side of the road just inside of Glaslyn and continues waving; I pull over too.

We both get out of our vehicles and without preamble he says, "John was shot. John isn't dead but it's pretty bad. I am a little shocked but compose myself quickly.

I say, "Curt, I know you like jokes but this isn't all that funny. And anyway," I continue, "if you were serious, you would be hugging me right now." As soon as I say this, like my dad would, he hugs me... and I know.

My knees start to buckle and tears come to my eyes. Avery opens the car window and looks in my direction. He and Austin see me and they start to freak out. I don't want to scare them so I force myself to stop.

We go to my friend Deedee's house in Glaslyn. Shawn- John's brother- phones me and tells me that John is in Meadow Lake. I am a little relieved because if it was life threatening, John would have been sent to the Royal University in Saskatoon.

My mom comes from Edam to Deedee's house. I tell everyone

present what Shawn said. I tell them my theory about Meadow Lake meaning that it's not that serious.

Then Shawn phones me back and says John is being taken to Saskatoon. I fall towards the floor and moan. Mom grabs the phone and explains to Shawn, "When she heard that she lost it."

***

Carol and Henry tell me that John was shot by a hunter who may have PTSD. His gun was loaded- he's not supposed to do that till he seems something to shoot.

When John went to check on him -as he is supposed to do- Al shot. He says he thought that John was a cougar... with thumbs.

Carol says, "The 300 Winchester magnum ballistic tip first hit him in his left thumb. It blew a huge whole in that finger and other fragments hit his index finger.

"Then it fragmented and ricocheted into his hip. It just missed his spleen and some arteries." If I get a chance, I will later tell him that he has an angel in heaven missing a thumb.

Henry continues for her, "Johnny ran away from Al in case he wanted to take a second shot. But when Johnny realized that he couldn't get back to the main road by himself, he went back to Al.

"Al said he would help so John climbed into the sleigh. But Al got the ski-doo stuck and in order to drive again, John had to pull himself out of the sleigh to drive out of the snowbank for Al."

Not too many men that have just had a hole blown in their side and finger could do that but John isn't just any-one.

*

John is about to go for surgery but first Dr. Keith, the surgeon, comes to talk to Carol and I in the waiting room. He says that John will probably live- you can't imagine the relief.

Further he says, "We're going to try to save his thumb but it doesn't look promising." John's thumb was all wrapped up when I saw him, so Carol shows me a picture of it; now I can see why. There is a hole bigger than a dime in it. The flesh is like hamburger.

I ask Carol to pray with me. We ask that no matter what happens God gets all the glory. I won't lie, if he dies I won't be quite as calm. And now we wait.

Dr. Keith reappears hours –or how long has it been? - later. He says that they were unable to save his thumb which is a little bit sad, but he continues:

"John's index finger also took some shrapnel and though we had to work at it, we saved it." I'm glad about the finger, a little sad about the thumb but nothing matters much because JOHN WILL LIVE.

I thank God for saving Him, but definitely don't dismiss the doctors' part. Thank God for their skills without who John would probably be missing his life, not just his thumb.

As soon as the doctor finishes and leaves, I get up, heading for the hallway. Carol comes half a step toward me and then stops. I say that I'm fine, I just need to be alone for a minute.

I should hug her- she almost lost her son so she must be feeling a million things- but I don't because I am not sure if she'd be okay with that- we are not touchy feely. So I walk around the corner, lean my back up against the wall and start humming "The Joy of the Lord is my Strength." The joy of the Lord *is* my strength.

Thank you so much Carol for staying with me for the first 12 days that John was in the hospital. You will never know how much it meant to me (and John of course) that you were there.

We had a routine while we were there... I'd sit in one of the waiting rooms and study statistics most of the day and you'd hang out and read and visit different parts of the hospital… and then we'd join up to see John again and then head to our inn.

You are one of the best parts of my life. You make me feel calm and in a world full of chaos. You will never know your value.

*

Thank you mom for supporting me and helping me through that time. She took me shopping a couple of days after John was shot -something I didn't feel interested in doing, but she must have known I needed it. She was there for us through it all.

*

Thank you Nikki. Though you might find this hard to recall, you comforted me. You tend to NOT be like that so I felt truly loved. And John was so happy to see you loving him. And Fabian- we love you.

*

Thank you Henry Sr, Shawn, Kristi, Caroline and Jr. You never left John's side. You stopped what you were doing to be with him (and I).

*

Thank you to all of our Four Square Church friends. You supported us prayerfully, financially and emotionally. Even though we'd only started attending a few months before John was shot. Thank you Pastor Dan going to the hospital. He will have a place in heaven for all of eternity, partly in due to you.

*

Thank you Denis and Bethany; Carla and Joel for inviting Avery and Austin into your homes while we were gone.

Getting them ready for school, housing them, getting them on the bus, comforting them while we were gone, would be hard. True friends don't always do the easy things but they do them none-the-less.

*

Thank you Deedee, Roy, Marleen, Randy, Joan, and all the rest of the Glaslyn Community Theatre Group. You stood there while I cried when I came to practice. Marleen, thank you for holding me while I did.

*

Thank you Jenine and David, Hali and John. For showing up at the hospital, for acting a little weaker than I'd expect you to which somehow made me feel a little stronger. Thank you for calming John (Koop) and easing his pain just by being there.

John (Wood), you might not recall but you called the morning after the accident (John was still in ICU though the two of you could converse). Even a complete mess, John was thrilled to talk to you. And one of the first things you talked about, even though you had just been shot by a *hunter* while *hunting*, was *hunting*! And somehow, I think that such normalcy is what John needed. And John Wood, I think talking like nothing had happened helped you process what happened to your best friend.

Hali and Jenine, we can't even express enough thanks for the benefit for John you spent hours planning and for hosting the big night! What's that saying, 'angels in disguise?'

UNIVERSE

The Sun shines upon my face,
Dries the tears from my eyes;
You bring me back to welcoming space
And Clear my cloudy skies.
Now moon beams bring me back my smile,
They show the dimples on my cheeks,
You take away this mind-wracking trial,
That has been going on for weeks.
If anyone tells me not to love you,
I look at the stars in the sky,
I know I love you so it's true,
I never want to say good-bye

WILL THAT REALLY CUT THE MUSTARD?

"... so you see, when it says that 'by His stripes we are healed' it isn't just that we're saved, it isn't just our souls and spirits." "Umm, I see," I say only half listening.

Lynn is really quite passionate, which is great, but I am not quite sure if she'd right in this instance. But I continue listening as she says, "Yep, He can heal us- better said, He DOES heal us. But sometimes our healing isn't quite the way we'd picture. Sometimes we're not healed till we die (in heaven everyone is healed).

Healing is super important, but Lynn seems oddly *too* interested in healing. As if we should automatically be healed just because Jesus died and rose again. For some reason that idea bothers me a tiny bit. Lynn doesn't notice my skepticism.

She continues: "I know, I can't believe everyone –including me- has had it so wrong for so many years. Jesus gave us authority and we just haven't been using it.

"We've been praying the wrong way and with no power. Jesus absolutely doesn't *want* us to be controlled by sickness or poverty in this world! But He can't do everything for us, we have to do some for ourselves! Alexis Kee"- she begins but I cut her off.

I ask, "Who is Alex whatever-her-name-is?" "Oh, this preacher that I listen to, she's so amazing! When she speaks it just resounds within me! She is such a woman of God! She found out the wonderful things God has for us *now*, not just in the future when we get to heaven.

"Alexis was saying that Jesus didn't mean for us to lose sight of the fact that the benefits to us of His sacrifice are more than just spiritual." "Hmm," I say, paying a little more attention. "It's something to think about.

"And I don't mean to cut you off or anything, but it's January 14th; John likes having an early tax call so I have to see when to ask for the tax consultant to come over."

***

"You know where it says in the Bible that if you have the faith of a mustard seed, you can say to this mountain 'be thrown into the sea!' and it will?" Lynn is at my house again today.

Currently I'm thinking about the bus that dropped the boys off after school almost an hour ago. They're not in the house yet and I think that I need to go call them in. As I head outside I shout to Lynn, because I don't want to sound rude, "I'll be right back but yeah, I know that verse."

"Well," Lynn starts again when I come back from yelling at the boys, "Jesus is saying that you have to believe for things to happen... wow, that sounded a little bit self-explanatory and obvious, didn't it?!" she laughs and I join in too.

Though sometimes she's a little too passionate, I can't dislike it too much because I'm that way about a lot of things myself. I am a little unsure about what she's saying but I *am* glad. It's great that she felt strongly enough to teach me what a lot of pastors don't mention!

"This is some good stuff," I say. "It makes sense that Jesus wouldn't just leave us on this Earth to go through the pain and agony of the fall and stuff. I've been studying the Bible for quite a few years but until you pointed this out to me I missed it!"

This 'have faith and it will manifest' thing is really starting to make sense to me. And she listens to this obviously really smart, insightful and godly Alexis woman whose teaching caused Lynn to see a new perspective and pointed it out to me. Lynn even lends me some of Alexis' many audio CDS and I love them.

Lynn also sometimes tells me about awesome faith stories: "There was this one guy, she once said, "Who had tumors on his chest. He just kept saying that he didn't have the tumors, even when he did. Then one day they were gone!"

Faith is to speak what is not as though it were. That's something Lynn told me... thankfully!

***

"Authority isn't really something I've thought a lot about before, you know? I mean, of course I love God and I seek Him all the time but now I have a more heightened point of view than I had.

"Now I know that just like we have to accept salvation –or believe, whatever- in order to be saved, we have to actually use our authority to claim by faith what is rightfully ours, such as healing or not accepting living poorer than we would like or whatever.

"And obviously," I continue, "when Jesus says He's given us all authority it has to mean our healing and things like that, right? I mean, it would be stupid to think that He has given us authority to just accept salvation and conquer over the devil."

I finish giving John my long spiel but I do so looking a little less certain of myself as when I began talking. But I am trying to get through his skull that he can claim his healing.

His side has been leaking gross discharge since he was shot. He changes bandages usually twice a day. You think he'd be eager to do the thing he should know makes sense.

It's not like I've just told him about this faith healing either.

Lynn joins me in it often. Two people making sense, how can he find justification to ignore that?

He just has to believe and he will probably be healed. It's probably part of his disbelief why he just seems not to care.

> Years ago my car had no radio. Well, it had one but it didn't work. I worked as a bartender in Edam once a week. To drive
> there takes about forty minutes from my house (or at least when I drive because I'm slow); I had lots of time to think.
> One day I drove past a cow on the side of the road. I see cows in the pasture alongside grid roads all of the time, it really wasn't noteworthy. All of a sudden, though, I had this resounding thought that said, "Life is simple, like a cow."

KICK THE CAN AND OTHER SUCH FUN

That creepy crawly feeling which my new neurologist said was Restless Leg Syndrome is back and it is worse. Even though I'm not pregnant.

It concerns me that whatever is wrong with me is changing -when I was pregnant I thought it was not that big of a deal because sometimes weird things happen when you're pregnant but this....

***

So after my appointment with the Edam doctor, I call John. I tell him, "The doctor in Edam is sending me to a specialist in Saskatoon."

"Well that's good, isn't it?" He says. I trust the doctor's judgement, especially since she's not a know-it-all. I'm hopeful about this Dr. Hunter guy that I'm going to see in a couple weeks.

***

I'm in his office. He says, "You know, sometimes you just have to be content with life and not make things up," Then he laughs out loud at my expense.

I can't believe that he seriously just laughed at me. I have spent the last five minutes telling him about my long (and verified) medical history and he dismissed me. I am distraught.

In hindsight, maybe anyone who hears me recite my history

–especially when you add in the fact that I am obviously dramatic- thinks I'm a little nuts.

Out in the waiting room, I grab John's arm. I look straight ahead and say, "Let's get out of here." In the parking lot, he asks me what the doctor said. "I'm too upset right now, I can't talk yet,"

We are five minutes out of Saskatoon when I tell John that the doctor laughed at me. Tears are now pouring down my face. It's another fifteen minutes before I say anything more.

John has not said anything since we left the doctor's office. He just keeps his hand on my back whilst I lie on the seat and inter- mittently weep.

Then without preamble I say, "I went into his office and waited for him to join me. When he appeared and introduced himself, I thought he seemed pretty nice. I mentioned to him about this creepy crawly feeling.

"Then he says that he can see from my chart I have quite a medical history. I thought that he sounded interested in helping me when he said 'quite a history!'"

I start crying afresh and John rubs my back and tells me it is okay. I cry for a few minutes and abruptly stop and I sit up.I wipe the tears from my eyes and I say with conviction, "Wait, that's okay. God will take care of it."

***

I followed up with the Edam doctor two weeks ago. I told her that Dr. Hunt seriously and literally laughed at me and dismissed me. She said that she had another doctor that she could call, a doctor Pat.

Now, July 13th, I'm in a room, waiting for Dr. Pat, neurologist, to come in. When she enters I think that she looks pretty nice –I think I'm generally a pretty good judge of character but then again, I thought Dr. Hunter looked nice and friendly too.

She looks at the chart like he had. Like him, she makes a note about my medical history, and then asks me to elaborate on it. She writes down everything I say, only stopping me occasionally to ask me questions. When she is done she looks a little miffed.

"So you say you've been on Lamictal for fourteen plus years now and you haven't had a single seizure that whole time?" "And," I throw in, "the phobia has been gone too. I think the Lamictal and Dilantin treated that as well."

"Here's the thing," she says a little hesitantly, "It is nearly impossible for a person with adult seizures to have no seizures for more than fourteen years." "But the Lamictal…," I say rhetorically. "No," she retorts kindly but authoritatively, "Even on seizure medication you'd still have the odd one, even if only small ones."

"Well, I'm a miracle," I say happily. I don't mention 'God' because I'm a little hesitant to do that in a doctor's office, but miracle implies His work. Suddenly Dr. Pat's countenance changes a little-she seems to become a little bit colder than a few seconds earlier.

I am quite sure that the face she is making means that she does not believe in God or hates God, or *something*. A feeling of anger wells up in me at her response; I think the feeling is 'righteous anger.'

I don't know for sure what to do, but I know that *something* must be done.

A SOMEWHAT
SCRATCHY
DEAD-HEAD

Lynn knows so much more than me. Still, there are brief moments where something inside of me thinks that this whole different kind of faith thing is too complex.

I think of Isaiah 55:8-9 which says that His ways and His thoughts are higher than ours. But this faith thing can't be wrong because there are people in this life that you just *know* are right. She is one of them.

Nearly every time I see her she tells me about the authority that we have as Christians. We don't need to have sickness or poverty. We as Christians have been waiting for Jesus to do everything for us.

She told me that some guy named Kenneth had a dream where Jesus told Him that he has to take charge of a certain situation, Jesus can't. So it's obvious then!

Sure, He answers prayers but we have to 'claim' things. For example, we need to say things like, 'I claim so and so's healing.' We also have to speak directly to our infirmities such as 'sore arm disappear' or 'thank you God that my arm is healed,' even if it's not but we hope it to be. We can't only rely on praying in the 'please do this for me Jesus' way.

There is no doubt that Lynn bends her knee –and I sure bend mine as well!- to Jesus. Of course we do, because our very breathing and being is found in Him.

Still, I'm a little confused about when we should pray or when to just claim what we need (ie: healing or poverty gone). I kind of wonder if all that Lynn has taught me –that she learned partly by attending Bible studies on healing at her church I think, and partly from listening to Alexis Kee- is too hard for me to do.

Should my 'prayer time' be kind of different than it currently is? And when I do pray, what exactly is it that I pray for? If I want my loved ones to be saved, do I just claim that it has happened even if I don't yet see it happening and then it will happen?

My saddest thought is that if I claim something and have faith in the 'not-yet-seen' and they don't manifest, it will mean my faith is not strong.

So maybe I will have failed God. That I'm pretty much just a low-life Christian?

ALL I DO IS WIND- STOLEN FROM SOME ELEVATED DUDE

Today is Wednesday, December 4th, 2013. On today's agenda is seeing Dr. Doppelman in North Battleford. I have a really bad, dry cough and my chest actually hurts. I think it's my chronic bronchitis acting up so though I'm not really concerned, I still feel the need to see the doctor (I know, I am neurotic).

When I get out of the Jeep the bitter cold chills me to the bone. Avery doesn't seem to think it's that bad. Inwardly I cringe because even my nine and a half year old is tougher than me.

Though when I have to half coax, half pull Austin out into the cold, I feel a little better. Not a lot, because he's just barely seven, but a bit. I guess living in Saskatchewan's cold and wind hasn't turned us all into crazy ice people.

I look over and see Austin standing on the sidewalk now, the little drama queen. At first he will do just about anything to stay in the Jeep, and now he's just standing still on the sidewalk with the wind lashing him.

He's staring at North Battleford city's Christmas decorations. Like he hasn't seen them before! I grab Austin's arm –I love that kid so much it hurts but it seems like I have to prod, coax, push or pull him all the time - and all three of us head to Dr. Doppelman's office.

We sit in the waiting room for a minute and then we're called in. The doctor says, "So what brings you in today Blaire?" Despite the fact he seems to have a 'Dr. Jekyll/Mr. Hyde' personality and can't seem to get me out of his office fast enough most of the time, he usually makes me smile –genuinely.

And he's one of the best doctors ever (don't tell him I said that, I'm sure there could be repercussions). He listens to and looks at me for only seconds before telling me that my throat is fine and, 'no, you do not need antibiotics.'

Then he shifts towards the computer and says that the neurologist I recently saw for my neck, Dr. Pat, sent him an email. He tells me that she wrote a short note about my neck.

The more interesting part, though, is when she addresses my seizures (not something she was seeing me for) and says, in what I imagine is a self-satisfied way, that I will never be off medication in my entire life. Not ever.

***

Prior to this moment I have never contemplated 'quitting' Lamictal. Now, though, that we are out of doctor Doppelman's clinic, I make up my mind.

She is challenging God's power and thereby insulting Him. I must defend Him the only way I know: by getting off my medication with the faith that He has healed me. I don't even need to consult anyone to do that.

***

I open the pill cupboard door. I shake my head a little at how many pills John and I have and think, 'well at least this will be one less!' I really intend to throw away my bottle of Lamictal.

For some reason, though, my hand won't pick the bottle up. I turn away in disgust, shutting the cupboard door a little too hard.

'Well,' I say, trying to placate myself, 'just because they're there doesn't mean that I'll ever use them again. And then after a few years they'll be so expired that I'll throw them out if nothing else for the reason that they're dusty and gross.'

***

"I just couldn't do it!" I sob to Lynn. After I had convinced myself I did not need nor would I ever again want my pills, I folded.

"I was overcome with anxiety –all created by me of course, thinking of open spaces and seizures. I couldn't stay off of them and though I felt outwardly better, inside I feel like the biggest failure."

Lynn has been listening patiently for several minutes and says, "That's okay Blaire, it really is, don't cry! You know, you probably just don't have enough faith for this right now and that's okay! We all have varying amounts of faith and yours is just maybe not mature enough yet."

"I feel so much better now that you have said that. Actually," I begin, "you know that Action Bible comic Bible that the boys have?

"Well, I just read out of the Action Bible devotional to the kids, the smaller copy that goes with the comic Bible. And the chapter we read was about Moses and God talking to him about speaking for the Israelites and all that.

"The key verse was, 'Now go, I will help you speak and teach you what to say.' Maybe it's like you said, that my faith isn't strong enough.

"But just like God wasn't mad at Moses for his human fear in going to speak to and for the Israelites, God isn't mad at me." "That's exactly right!" she says.

DESPERATE NEW HOUSE WIVES OF EDAM

It's December 2014; we just arrived at Koop's house. Two of John's aunties- Mariann and Sheran- are here. Almost as soon as we get upstairs, they tell me to lie on the floor.

Less than three months after trying to go off my pills, John and I decided to have another baby and voila, he or she is almost here!

So Mariann and Sheran are about to swing a pin on a string over my belly, a supposed surefire method to reveal baby's sex. The pin indicates another boy but it sure doesn't feel like it. Granted it was a while ago that the boys were born, but this whole pregnancy is so different, especially because it feels like this baby is living in my ribs.

My caesarian section is booked for January 29, 2015 which is good because I'm about ready to have this baby out! I don't think I'd want another ten and a half pounder like I did with Avery, or one with a head as big as Austin's. Getting it out soon sounds good to me!

I smile to myself for another reason too: it wasn't too long after I became pregnant that I decided in my mind that I was going to go off my pills again. This time for good and with no doubts, as soon as this pregnancy is over.

I haven't told anyone other than Lynn about my plans. I'm sure that if I told just about anyone my plan, they'd back me… but I don't plan on telling anyone else.

Especially not John because I am sure that he wouldn't understand.

***

I never cried when I first saw Avery or Austin for the first time. I mean, it was exciting and wonderful, but no tears. Seeing Elle, my daughter, for the first time brings on the waterworks. John asks, "Blaire, what's the matter?" as if he doesn't know; well maybe he doesn't, but 'duh!'

***

We've been home for 6 days now. Mom is here cooking and cleaning and visiting. This is my third child, but it's still hard to imagine doing laundry and cooking and breastfeeding and changing diapers and trying to squeeze sleep in there too!

Even though I'm busy with Elle, I can't stop thinking about getting off my pills. I'll do it in about a week. After a good year or two off the pills, I'll tell John and it will probably build his faith.

I can't wait for the testimony it'll be to everyone else too when they hear! Gotta have authority, right?

***

I'm standing at the pill cupboard with no doubts in my mind. Elle's now eight days old. I grab the bottle of Lamictal and in one swift motion I open the lid, open the cupboard under the sink and toss the pills into the compost pail.

When I stand up I feel resolved and strong and in control. I know that I will never again need those pills. My faith has made me well. What kind of life is it if you're chained to pills or some other substance instead of claiming the rights that we have?

I am not passive in this Christianity game. I'm thinking about how the devil has been defeated in my life and I'm a little gleeful. I feel, somehow, more in the spiritual 'loop.' To think, this all was prompted by a doctor that needed spiting for insulting God.

***

Lynn is at my house today and amongst other things, we discuss 'faith.' We are currently discussing the different people that need to have more faith in order to be healed –not me, I already did that.

The first person we discuss is John, of course. In the years since he was shot, his side has never healed or stopped draining. I think John has just accepted that he has this wound and that's going to be the way it is. Yes, I know God sometimes talks about accepting our lot in life but we need to speak to our mountains.

Lynn and/or I often back up belief leading to healing by quoting scriptures. He just always says that I am taking them out of context. It's like he isn't interested in being made whole. He has to realize that like the woman who bled for twelve years, he must be healed from the source.

John says that there are reasons we can't understand why God doesn't heal every *one*, every *time*. He insinuates that Lynn and I are trying to play God- how infuriating! Lynn also tells him that sometimes he must do more than claim, that he needs to fast.

BIRDSONG

Bluebirds of joy sing sweetly to me,
Calming all my fears.
Let the notes carry me from this terrible sea
That's been causing all my fears.

But as the Bluebirds call my name,
I just hear the crows,
Things will ever be the Same,
And my darkness Grows.

Oh putrid tears that steal my soul.
Where once was a heart is now a hole.
The Wrath thrown upon my burdened heart,
Leaves me with just reason to depart.

Because I am the cause for Your tears coming down,
Stealing your smile with a replacing frown,
I am the reason you laugh no more,
I scare you to death with my ominous roar.

So if I was to leave I'd do justice to you,

Making all of your dreams and hopes come true,
Your heart would soar like the clouds in the sky,
And you would rejoice the absence of i.

"ARIEL, JUST TELL THE BOY THAT YOU'RE THE GIRL UNDER THE SEA"

Elle –my little girl- is nearly one. It has been a good year at home with her, but I am possibly starting a new job with my newly-acquired Bachelors of Science in Psychology.

The counselling job interview today is at a North Battleford sexual assault centre. First, though, I am going to give my testimony at a Catholic High School.

***

I'm done my spiel at the North Battleford high school. I'm exiting the school and I have the weirdest sensation. I also had that same weird sensation walking down the school hallway to the classroom where I would give the presentation.

I don't think it's nerves but I can't place it, either. Oh well, I head off to the sexual assault centre for my interview. The executive director is a gentleman named Norman who, at the end of the interview, hires me.

I am extremely pleased; I feel like a true professional. Oh, by the way, that weird feeling: it disappeared only a few minutes after I got out of the school. Weird but I am quite sure it won't happen again.

***

I've been a counsellor for over a month now. I absolutely love it here –or more exactly, what I'm doing. Though life seems great now, the uncomfortable feeling that I got several weeks back returns a couple of times a week for brief seconds. Nothing comes from those moments, but I can't say I enjoy them.

***

I've been here for several months now and I find that the feeling is getting worse. Six months ago I couldn't place it nor recognize any sort of pattern; now I kind of do.

Spaces that are really big –like gymnasiums or parking lots or crossing the street- make me feel this weird uncomfortable feeling that permeates my whole entire brain and body.

When the fear of those large, open spaces hits, I can think of little else. I just think about getting from the place I'm *at* to a *safe place* (ex: a chair, a door frame, a person, anything I can sit on, stand near or grab onto).

***

I was full time at the sexual assault center for nearly a year and a half. Several months ago I asked to be moved to part time work so I wouldn't have to travel quite as often to North Battleford.

Unfortunately, I just got laid off for it; my boss said there's not enough work and the part time worker must be the first to go. This sucks for me because I love my job. More than that, I had the most clients in my office so I hope they don't suffer as well.

But maybe the extra time I will get to rest, because of unemployment, will resolve the anxiety thing that I am feeling. I have been getting too little sleep since starting at the center- having to get up at night with Elle most nights, getting up early, cleaning and cooking when I get home and then having to find time to spend with the kids and husband.

Maybe this will give needed respite from being scared of open spaces. The fear, as well, no longer is limited to only *some* spaces like big parking lots.At this point, it is pretty much anything and everything. I am now terrified when in carpeted hallways, small offices, you name it.

Now what I think are panic attacks are beginning to manifest in physical attacks of some sort. When my fear of open spaces reaches a climax, I fly into flight-or-fight mode and stop thinking. I freeze for one to three seconds in the middle of whatever I'm doing and just kind of stare. I can see, but I can't really move.

During these attacks I can hardly even think. Prior to it happening, I tell myself that as long as I am rational when I'm in an open space, I'll be ok. I tell myself to think logically about the fact that nothing is really going to hurt me.

When I am *actually in* an open space, though, my brain starts to unravel which triggers an attack. I so want to give in to reason but instead I just give in to madness.

Since this has got to be merely psychological, relaxing will probably fix me. Or at least I'll hold onto the faith it will, and then it probably will.

I have started occasionally thinking –to my own chagrin- that these attacks have something to do with seizures. The seizures that Dr. Pat said would never go away without medication. I can't admit that out loud to anyone though, not even to my own self.

If these are seizures, treating them might treat the fear. I was fearful when my seizures weren't controlled as a teenager but as soon as they were, the fear lessened until it was gone all together.

But Lynn would likely be disappointed if I resorted to seeing a doctor. And seeing someone would be something like uprooting what I have already claimed, wouldn't it?

I don't want to fail again. On the other hand, I'm starting to wonder if needing medication for a medical problem is really failing at all?

I do have some other good reasons, though, for *not* wanting to take medication. It ties you down: you need to have it with you or be home to have it at a certain time.

There are other reasons too, but right now I can mostly only think of how I can't let Dr. Pat win. I am so confus*ing* as well as plain confus*ed*, but I can't stop these thoughts. I need God to help me but I don't know what I need Him to help me with exactly.

Anyway, relying on Him is hard right now. He doesn't seem to want the best for me or else I wouldn't even *be* in this situation.

So at the moment, I stand in the middle of a rock and a hard place- literally, *the Rock* and a hard place.

***

"I'll come help you, and Elle can tag along too. It would be so nice if I could actually get something done without having to drag along a kid but I guess that's what you get," I spit out.

I then continue, "It's too hot to have to climb into the back seat to get a kid into their car seat but whatever." I hate life, everyone and everything. Everyone is an inconvenience and I have no patience. And you need patience for a 3 year old.

I swear, that's part of the reason that Elle drives me absolutely bonkers. I mean, she's really cute and I really love her, but she whines and cries and is so bossy. John is just about as bad.

That's not to say that Elle is *never* fun. Sometimes there are moments of reprieve. Sometimes we are happy together. Occasionally she doesn't tell me I'm playing the wrong way in a game that I'm only playing because she asked me to play in the first place.

Sometimes she doesn't scream and yell. Sometimes she cuddles up so cute on the couch with John and me and her brothers. Sometimes things almost feel normal.

And I realize it is not totally her fault that I am not patient enough. I occasionally think that I'd be more patient if I was back on seizure medications.

I got really grouchy years ago while I had the accidental overdose. After it, I found that I was much grouchier than when I was younger, but the (correct) dose of pills seemed to help.

I have free-will choice, but I've started to feel that I can't choose as much as I earlier thought. Especially when nothing I do or think stops, or even alters, the attacks that make my right side now go numb and right toes to curl.

What I can choose, I think, is kind of like an armless person wanting to play football. Even if they tried really hard, they probably would never be able to play (without prosthetics, of course). Maybe it's like trying to make red, blue and vice versa.

***

I'm hanging laundry on the deck outside. I am terrified, wondering if I'll get through this. John's truck pulls into the driveway and before I know it, he's at the steps. He asks me to join him for some reason so I head toward him.

That's when it happens: pushing myself away from the railing, where I hang clothes, causes an have an attack or seizure or whatever it is: my face freezes and I feel it tense up into something like a snarl. The toes on my right foot curl and my right foot jerks upwards a few inches. John sees it all.

It only lasts about four seconds but long enough –not to mention my rabid look- that I know there is no brushing it off as stubbing my toe. Before John can say anything, I tell him that I have little panic attacks but it's no big deal.

John's face tells me he knows, though, that it *is*. He asks, "How long has this been happening Blaire?" "Oh," I pause and pretend that I don't know for certain before saying, "probably a year or so. Maybe less." I think he is shocked that I never told him.

"And how often does that happen Blaire?" he inquires further but I hesitate a second before answering. I have convinced myself, in the past three-ish years of basically lying to John, that I was doing nothing wrong in not telling him.

I reasoned that he didn't need to know because it was going to go away right away anyway. Really, I know that I have just been too prideful and self-righteous to tell him.

That is my thought in that split second; that is the reason I don't reply to his question right away. I know that he knows that I know I should not have done what I did.

Trying to sound blasé I reply, "Three to five a day." Though John is hiding quite well how stunned he is that I never told him till he caught me, I can see it in his eyes. They show me his hurt and his anger.

The words, 'Ariel, just tell the boy that you're the girl under the sea' appear in my mind.

AIRPLANE

The storm grapples
With your mind
But not My mind.
because My mind is Mine.
I won't ever forget that
so mind yourself.
Grapple all You want
but I won't lose because my fight
Has been fought;
I won.
I battled;
I battled always. Did.
I said No.
No. I will not be a Victim
Of My own Mind.
there are stories to tell,
Tears to cry but No longer for Pain,
No More. I Won.
because I Refused to Be
Victimized, to be Trampled upon,

By My own Pain. Thoughts.
I'm Free. But it'll cost. You.
So free, Much More than I ever
thought I'd be.
so your grappling storms
In Your mind
Aren't mind.
so Mind.

BUY, DON'T JUST BROWSE

I am browsing the internet when I come upon an article about anxiety and seizures. The article details a woman who, in her youth and also in her adulthood, had occasional 'panic attacks.'

She was told that these attacks took place because she had a weak constitution and anxiety issues. She believed this to be true, partly because she had nothing to suggest otherwise.

Then one day she found out that she had a type of seizure in which there is something like a visual aura of fear or anxiety. The doctors treated them; she felt not only physically better but reassured that she wasn't imagining things.

I don't think I found this article by accident.

The biggest city I generally drive in has a population of only about twenty thousand people. Bigger cities scare me: navigating through multiple lanes while trying to follow maps or directions and not hit other cars flusters me greatly.

I had to drive myself through Saskatoon a few years ago

and while it is definitely not huge, it has all the elements I freak out at (and about 200,000 people).

About ten minutes before entering the city, I became sweaty and my heart started pounding in my head and chest. I knew I needed to remember to be rational. I reminded myself that nervous symptoms (like heart beating fast) are irrelevant to safety.

I took steps to alleviate as much stress as possible: getting into the right lane long before a turn; turning the radio off so as to think as clearly as possible; not second-guessing the GPS that my husband programmed for me.

I drove proactively and got in and out of the city uneventfully. But it wasn't just being proactive that helped me. I prayed just about the whole way through. But one might say, 'it was your actions that got you through and that was all' and I would partially agree.

But while I was busy praying, I wasn't so focused on me. While I was busy praying, God was helping me listen to my GPS's instructions even though panic made me want to take the wrong turns.

God helped me remember to get in the right lane with lots of time to spare so that I didn't stress as much.

God is a part of your life, all of the time.

I am sitting in my church chair, surrounded by beautiful happy Christmas decorations but feel neither beautiful nor happy. I am going to have to talk to people and I will have to pretend I'm okay when I am terrified nearly all the time.

My brain hurts from how foggy it is; I'm only 35, this shouldn't be happening; how am I going to be able to walk through the church foyer and parking lot when the sermon finishes?

I hate that I hate nearly everything and I have no ambition and am unbelievably distraught and defeated. I hate that I have to appreciate that I am no longer working because, as much as I loved it, it was getting too hard for me (and admitting that out loud makes me sound bad).

I hate that I don't even feel like I love people that I've always loved. I want to want to be with Elle and I want her to want to be with me, but all of this *wanting* is not amounting to much.

I feel like God has abandoned me all over again because I can't remember that He *never did* the first time.

Depression is the worst guilt, shame, self-loathing, feeling of worthlessness and monster dread anyone can ever feel. Depression is not sadness- one can realize their life is pretty darn good and blessed and still be utterly depressed.

My 'seizure/anxiety' predicament did not make me depressed but I have been depressed -as well as sad, constantly sad- in the past few years.

Depression is horrid; the only thing that saved me from depression was plastering my life with reminders of the Word and seeking God.

Such as the verse in the Bible where the Apostle Paul says it is better for him to stay in this world to tell others about Jesus than go to heaven right now.

It is not a verse about suicide and depression but one day in 2018 –a day with no depression but depression was recently on my mind- I read that verse and it was a 'eureka'.

Paul would have loved to go to heaven right then to be with God but being here was more beneficial for the kingdom, even if it wasn't more beneficial for him.

Suicidal thoughts are desires to get out of this world because you just want to escape *it*.

You think that there is nothing good about you being alive and that everyone would be better off without you.

That is *not* meant to sound insulting to those who are or have been suicidal or to their
friends of families.

But when those feelings come that, as far as I can tell, you can't help, try to hold on to the above thought.

And it sounds inconsiderate to tell you of your *duty* when you feel like total crap. But, while we don't "owe" God (we don't live by works –Ephesians 2:8-9), we do "owe" God.

We owe Him to stay here and shine our light (Matt. 5:16), even if we don't think we have much of a light to shine.

We owe him because that's our purpose. And in shining what little you have left, your light might break your own storm.

***

The service finishes and my pastor invites anyone who wants prayer to stay in the sanctuary. He doesn't usually do this so I feel it's kind of a sign... or something.

It seems like a sign because two weeks ago, for no reason I can understand, I made an unspoken request on a Facebook prayer group. My cousin, a church friend and my school friend are part of that group and they reached out to me.

I told them that I'm extremely mad and then I am depressed about being so mad and depressed. I said that I have no idea what's wrong with me but I know I need help. They consoled me and said they would pray. For some reason I think this might be their prayers answered.

When I look up, my pastor is in front of me, waiting for me to speak. I ask him to pray for something about my phobia.

I am so conflicted that I hardly make sense. My words are a whispered cry that I didn't even know were in my throat until I open my mouth.

♩ BLUE, OH SO LONELY FOR LOVING YOU ♩

It's Saturday, six days later. Last night –or this morning- I woke up and had a sudden revelation that I need to see a doctor.

I need to tell he or she everything, and get a prescription for Lamictal (I still get over-obsessed with controlling my own life, I realize this).

***

The first day I took Lamictal © I couldn't stop blinking and I could barely stay awake. I napped on the couch for an hour. That was 6 days ago and already I'm having fewer attacks –or seizures or whatever. Now it's only two and sometimes even only one.

Maybe God is using Lamictal. Although just thinking that makes me feel guilty. Something must be terribly wrong with me that I didn't have enough faith to be healed, pure and simple. Or is it that simple?

> I have balked at reading the psalms. Most of them seemed too hopeful to be good or real.
> Like seriously, who praises God when they're being

attacked by their own son –David and Absalom? That sort of thing.

Over the past few years I've realized that not yet seeing your solution is not mutually exclusive with praising the one who can but is not yet giving it. I hope that happens if I ever start plummeting again.

So I immersed myself in Psalms. Particularly Psalm #91 which is about favor and supernatural protection.

Verse 14 says, "Because he has loved Me, therefore I will deliver him; I will set him securely on high, because he has known My name."

He takes care of us when we stop holding on to all control.

We get the 'best' of God when we give Him ours.

Sometimes, even though the problem is still there, it seems a little smaller because we realize we are not alone.

***

I've been on Lamictal for several months. I am now only having one, maybe two 'things' a day but the terror has not lessened one iota. John and I stand in the kitchen, me clinging to him for dear life.

I had believed that by taking medication I was letting Lynn down. I thought that not only would I be letting her down, I would be admitting that I was not as good as her. I would be admitting that I was a loser. I mean, I'd have to be if I couldn't even manage 'word of faith' correctly.

So standing there I scream to him, "I never want to speak to her again! Lynn should have known that I was so vulnerable! "She should have known that someone who's been on medication most of her life would be talked out of taking her medication if told about 'name it and claim it' crap enough!" (I've found out that the 'name-it-and-claim-it, have-faith-in-what-is-not-seen-

and-God-will-do-just-about-anything' line of thought is called the faith, or word-faith, or word-of-faith movement) (ie: Hanegraff, 1993; Mattera 2013; Wikipedia Word of Faith, 2015).

"She should have known that she couldn't put God in a box like she did! We can't just say that we want things to happen and think that they will and that if they don't we're insufficient in some way!

"I know I don't really have a right to say this after all I fell for but still! And I feel so insufficient and I hate it! God is the giver of all good gifts and who's to say that the good gift will always look good to us?

"Maybe my medication –though it seemed bad to Lynn and people like her- was one of God's ways of being good to me. You know how I mention Lamentations chapter 3 a lot?" I ask John. "Ummmm, remind me," he says like when he doesn't have a clue what I am talking about.

"Jeremiah wrote Lamentations," I start to say but John looks at me a little blankly. It could be for a variety of reasons such as him having no clue who Jeremiah even is. Or maybe he already knows but I just don't know he knows because he takes weird pleasure in having me think he doesn't know when he does.

I continue: "He was a prophet of Israel." I get no response from John such as, 'Oh, now that you mention Jeremiah I definitely re-member Lamentations 3!' so I sigh and shake my head. "Anyways," I go on, "he laments over how Israel has left God and how God has'broken her teeth' by sending her into captivity in Babylon.

"And then Jeremiah says, 'Do not both good and evil go forth from God?' He says that since we are the clay why we would judge what the potter is doing. We can ask God questions and He can handle our anger and fear and pain but we shouldn't think that we can tell Him what to do.

"People don't always or even often know the will of God. Word faith people always say it's not the will of God for any Christian to be sick. But look at verses like Isaiah 55:8-9 which says that God's thoughts" –but I am cut off by John who says: "-are not our thoughts and His ways are not our ways."

I'm momentarily speechless because that's exactly right. John might have read that in the Bible. Or he might have been listening to me one of the many times I've quoted it. Either way, I'm impressed.

I say, "Still, this hurts so much John! I am terrified of everything! I can't go anywhere! I was her guinea pig and wittingly or not, she took advantage of me! She sat in her ivory castle tenting her fingers evilly and laughing to herself because she could test out her word-faith crap that she was learning!"

He only speaks to tell me that she wasn't intentionally evil to me. I say, "Oh fine, but it's still a possibility!" I feel empty. I don't plan to tell her that I am not nor was I *ever* healed of seizures. I don't plan to tell her about the phobia.

People like her wouldn't listen to reason if it slapped them in the face. Besides, I don't think she deserves to know... nor do I think that I should have to go through the pain she will inevitably give me for saying I'm on medication again.

She will never be convinced that word-faith is not a thing. Part of the reason I know this is that any time I raised any doubts about word-faith, she shut them down.

She was busy selling something she wanted to be true. I don't need her guilt and condemnation and mind control. She doesn't even deserve to know what I think of her right now nor maybe ever. I have never had a terribly hard time with forgiveness.

I don't think I can forgive this though. No one else I've been mad at and then forgiven has ever been the driving force in hurting me this much.

Humility.

Once, a few years ago, I wrote a book called ABAN-
DONED BY YOU. It was a lot like this book. Actually, it was
exactly like this but for two things: #1 the editing (the syntax,
grammar, layout and some tone). Reason #2 is where humility
comes in.

A few months into writing the book, Lynn told me her
'idea'- the word of faith, 'name it claim it', 'just wish and believe you are healed' thing.

Of course, when I went off my medication, I wrote it into
the book. I wanted everyone to believe what I had been so
lucky to be taught.

Well, as it so wonderfully turned out, the seizures were
NOT gone and I DID need medication.

God HAD performed a miracle for me through my pills,
letting me have NO seizure activity while on my pills, but the
miracle still required them to be part of my life (maybe that
was also part of keeping me humble? And the fact that in this
imperfect, fallen world I acquired cancer which I had chemo
for which can have bad effects, such as seizures)

I didn't want ANYONE to listen to my 'advice' gleaned
from the advice I took from Lynn, and have the same down-
fall- I am not just talking about getting sick by going off
necessary meds or treatment but of being pained because I
lessened God to make me seem bigger (see Luke 17:1-2 for an
example of making someone stumble).

So I got my publisher to remove ABANDONED BY YOU
from the market. And yes, in theory it is so easy to say this
was a great and very easy process, that would be a bit of a lie.
The crow that I had to eat was a very hard time in my life.

I finally realized my error and that I must tell others that my pride went before my fall.

There *are* individuals with the gift of faith –you know those gifts of the Spirit? Ex: see 1 Corinthians 12 and part of 13). Some have it but to some, that's not what God has given them.

I do not have a gift of faith. I have faith that God, though I don't see Him, is there. Partly because of what He does and partly because in myself I just know in the way we all feel but don't necessarily act on (Romans 1).

But that doesn't even totally matter. Because it was my crazy thoughts that led me to make a crazy choice. Whether I did or did not have faith was beside the point.

Those with the gift of faith don't just believe that what they want is what God will do and then God does it. No, I think they have insight from the Holy Spirit saying that God WANTS and WILL do a particular thing, something in their soul tells them this and then they have FAITH that it will happen and it does.

I very truly hope that my story might make you think twice before making a horrible decision like I did.

It is always very possible that God will completely and immediately heal someone. Other times, though, it might be through medication or through a therapy or something like that.

If He decides to do the former, you will probably hear it from Him rather than just wish it. Maybe the same with the latter.

If you think you're one of the ones that God has healed,

goodie... but don't just quit your medication or therapy. Consult a doctor first to see where your health is at.

God made medication and doctors and medical tests for a reason. If your x-ray shows that your heart is 100% when it was failing a month ago or that your medication levels show you to be in the toxic range and you need to go down or off, THEN do what the doc says... or something like that.

So about my book again: the publisher pulled it. I decided to totally revamp (and rename) the book (what I've been doing for the last couple of years). So though it's a true story, I wrote it twice. And it's humbling.

BARRED IN

i sit in this cold
stone walled Prison.
the only things I
receive are
bread crumbs and warm
water.
you reach your hand out to me
As far as it will go
But you can't reach me
'if i tried a little harder'
you say, 'I could
break free'
But how do you break free
from something that's Part
of you?
something implanted onto your
Mind
can you?
all around me people play
they beckon me to

break Free.
but i can't.
i'm bound by ropes and chains.
bound by my Thoughts

SPEAK UP!

John doesn't come to church with me as much as I'd like. As far as I know, he rarely reads his Bible; yes, I read *to* him but he doesn't really listen, something he sometimes admits.

He doesn't initiate conversations about God and he participates as little as possible in the ones we do have. And, I often wonder if he ever praises God, especially out loud.

The thing is, maybe singing a song to God isn't the only praise (and I say that rhetorically and a little sarcastically because of course it's not). He has praised God in many other ways.

Sometimes I voice (well, I don't do this much anymore) my confusion and doubts to him about my medication. I asked him something about 'maybe is going on Lamictal wrong and giving up on God?'

He always replies, "God healed you by giving you Lamictal. End of story." Is he right?

I heard a Max Lucado quote recently that says, "love like there is no tomorrow and if tomorrow comes, love anyway" (2007). Trust that God can heal and even if He doesn't, keep loving and trusting. And definitely don't make everything about the healing.

Let's look at a Biblical story of healing (or better put, un-healing). The Apostle Paul was given "a thorn in the flesh" (2 Corinthians 12:7a). We don't know exactly what it was, but he said it was "a messenger of Satan to torment me... to keep me from exalting my-self" (2 Corinth. 12:7b).

God wouldn't take it away. There are often different reasons, but in this instance, it was for humility. If the Apostle Paul –the guy who God inspired to write over half of the New Testament- had to have a 'thorn in the flesh' to keep him humble, why do I (or you) think I (we) don't?

One of my favorite chapters in the Bible is similar to Paul's thorn- it is Lamentations 3. Jeremiah is complaining how God has crushed Israel (and by proxy, him).

He says that it seems God revels in their/his pain. But then he says that sometimes he has to moan a bit but he realizes he's just spouting. He says that he knows he is the clay and God is the potter. Jer. 3:38says that both good and ill go forth from the hand of God.

It's one of my favorite chapters because it gives me a strange hope (although I don't really think it's strange at all). If pain comes from God then there's a purpose to it –Satan might be the one to cause the pain sometimes –the other times we do it ourselves- but it is only because God allows Him to.

God didn't *make* me choose to get off my pills, catapulting me into years of pain. He knew that I would make that choice yet He gave me the opportunity anyway.

He knew that I'd take the word-faith bait. He wanted me to learn to love Him independent of Him fixing all of my problems (well, I'm learn*ing*) (and let's not be hypocritical and say that He is so selfish. Parents do that to their kids... and secondly and more importantly, we don't often know why God does what He does).

When God plans something -or is in some way involved- why should we hate it? Not forgiving Lynn was to disregard that God had

a plan. I decided I needed to do that. I doubt I will ever have the relationship with Lynn that for so many years we did, but I have to forgive her.

As you might have heard Corrie Ten Boom (and others) say before,

> Unforgiveness is a prison. Those who were able to forgive their former enemies were able also to return to the outside world and rebuild their lives, no matter what the physical scars. Those who nursed their bitterness remained invalids. It was as simple and as horrible as that."
> (Ten Boom, C., November 1972).

The Bible says that if we forgive others, our Heavenly Father will forgive us (ex: Matt. 6:14-15). Forgiveness also cleanses us from all unrighteousness (1 John 1:9).

Without forgiveness the Holy Spirit can't fully dwell in us (Acts 2:38). We know that the Holy Spirit is the comforter, the teacher and the counselor so we don't want to be without that!

James 5:16 even says that forgiveness heals us. According to Proverbs 28:13 it even causes us to prosper and receive mercy.

It is hard to forgive. But unforgiveness is, as we have also heard many times, like drinking poison and waiting for your enemy to die. It is hard because Satan tells us they don't deserve it and it will be bad for us. It is hard because sometimes it seems impossible to even find it in yourself to start trying. But God lives in us to give us the strength (ex: Philippians 2:13 and 4:13).

PATTY-CAKE, PATTY-CAKE, BAKER MAN

"I really don't even know if there's a point in going." He is about to cut me off but I continue, "I know, I know, saying I'll submit to God doesn't mean much if it's just words.

"I *apparently* actually have to take the first step of trusting that He has good reasons for making me do certain things. But I don't want to see her if all she's going do is gloat. I mean, what else is she going to do?"

"Well, she might tell you why you're dizzy and shaking and nauseous and why you can't shut up" -I shoot him a very dirty look before he laughs and continues, "I mean, about when you told me you can't stop yourself from speaking inanely to people and you feel high.'

Although," he spits out quickly and with a laugh, "you *are* kind of a mouth piece in general… even when you're not feeling like you're high."

I'm about to react to the whole 'mouth piece' thing but he wraps his arms around me and pulls me onto his lap to show he's only teasing.

With his arms still around me I say, "It's just a lesson in being embarrassed… but I don't like needing lessons." I'm only half serious because I know that I need to see Dr. Pat.

For months -heck, a couple years is more like it- I've had this inkling that seeing Dr. Pat is what I'm being led to do. She's a really good neurologist and I need someone really good.

There's one other problem that any other doctor could probably deal with, but like I said, she's one of the best. The problem has to do with Dilantin©.It was the drug I took alongside Lamictal© when my seizures stopped at age 16.

While the seizures and fear have lessened a little bit -which I am very happy about- I have some bad side effects. I shake most of the time, am often nauseous, often can't stop myself acting strange and I have a very sore liver (and since I'm already missing 1/3 of it from cancer, I don't need to further hurt it).

***

It's November 23rd and John and I are in Saskatoon in Dr. Pat's office. We wait less than a minute and Dr. Pat enters. She looks no different than when I saw her nearly seven years ago.

She asks me what is going on. I tell her a little bit of what's transpired in the past five and ¾ years. That my current meds are Lamictal© and Dilantin© and about my nausea, shaking, talkativeness and my sore liver.

Immediately (and I am not being overdramatic here) she says that I am having Dilantin© toxicity. This actually makes sense to me; I am on a fairly high dose (400 mg/day).

What I am not expecting, though, is that she tells me to get off it. This is somewhat reminiscent of Dr. Dewitt. She also says, "Instead we're going to do" -she doesn't say 'try' as if there's any chance of it not working- "Keppra©. It is a good medication for you because it is processed through your kidneys, not your liver."

"I told you seven years ago that you needed seizure medication.

Keppra© has been found to be quite effective for your type of sei-zures -seizures that begin in the frontal lobe but then quickly move to include your temporal lobe as well."

My brain is a little overwhelmed by how quick and maybe well this is going, and partly by the little 'jab' that she oh-so-subtly-but-really-not-subtly inserted into our conversation.

I quickly forget, though, because I hear her say that if an EEG machine was put on my head when I have the periods (many peri-ods) of panic, it would be able to read that those were seizures, just like the ones that are visible.

That is basically what I have been waiting for, for years. I have worried that I have just worried myself into a phobia. Now I hear her say that I am not responsible for *some* (maybe not all because part of it is my doing) of the anxiety. The seizures and phobia *are* related, like I've thought for a very long time.She says, "And after tonight no more Dilantin© and start Keppra© tomorrow morning."

***

Once John and I are back in the truck I start crying. "What's the matter?" John asks, somewhat confounded, "Isn't what she said to you a good thing?

"She knew right away what you weretalking about when you said you were nauseous and dizzy and talkative and your brain was on fire."

"I know, I am happy, I am. It's just that I'm also freaked out because the Dilantin was sort of working and now what if the Keppra© doesn't and then"- but John cuts me off.

"How about we just wait and see."

THINGS RESEMBLING HEART SHAPES

Today is April 8th 2021. It has been nearly 6 years since I quit taking my seizure medication. It has been nearly 2.5 years since I began taking them again and approximately 6 months since I started Keppra©.

There is no doubt that this has been very trying for me, but it has been possibly harder on our family as a unit. Or rather, I have been.

First and foremost I thank God for John. I don't know how he forgave me (so quickly I think) for hiding a health condition for 3 years.

He has also dealt with me screaming and yelling that my brain is on fire; being sad and sometimes even depressed; and making claims that invisible things (open spaces) are terrifying.

That's not even anywhere nearly as bad as the whole 'word of faith' stuff that I tried stuffing down his throat. The accusations that he wasn't healed because he didn't believe enough.

Insinuations that he was faithless and that Lynn and I were better than him in some way. Of me ignoring his admonitions that the whole 'word of faith' thing that I was feeding him was unbiblical.

I've hardly stopped to empathize with *his* personal burden from the gun-shot. He has hardly complained for the 9 years that he's been changing bandages and going to doctors. He hasn't griped about the injustice of *that*.

There are so many things I could say about John but I can't really form words. Let's just say that he lives out 1 Corinthians 13 better than anyone I've ever met.

I sometimes think he's Hosea and I'm Gomer... sort of anyway.

******

Avery and Austin are amazing. They are so strong and dependable. They take care of their mama and are as kind as it's possible for teenage boys to be. They work their butts off but they still make time for us.

Avery is deep and thoughtful and strong and dependable. When I have felt horrid over the years, he has never acted disrespectful or resentful.

He lets me kiss him and hug him and tell him how much I love him; He lets me call him my beautiful boy (by John Lennon and heard by me on Mr. Holland's Opus).He even smiles a bit though he tries to hide it. I think it means more to me than to him, and I eat it all up.

***

Austin hugs me and tells me that he loves me. I don't think he's ever told me to just go away when I tell him that I am scared of the open spaces. He stands beside me and pats me on the back and says, "I'm here Blaire" (we are working on getting him to call me mom!

He also has a song that he lets me sing to him: Everything I do I do it for you (I was born in the 1980s and it shows).

Without Austin's love and forgiveness in the past 5 years, I don't know if I could have made it. He has heard me scream when I was frustrated and couldn't think (thankfully this happens only rarely now).

That kid has seen his mama at her very worst –more than Avery *or* Elle have- but he doesn't give up on me- or at least I don't think so and I definitely hope not!He is strong and mature and dependable and creative and a million other awesome things.

If I've messed you up Austin, I beg your forgiveness. I also pray, pray, pray that this doesn't stick with you. It is not one's fault when someone else acts crazy… except when John makes me act crazy!

******

I still struggle with being patient, and am often annoyed by Elle's confounding bossiness and what seems to me a little entitlement.

She is so obviously a youngest child but add to that that she's also sort of an only child with Avery and Austin being so much older than her. Still, as frustrated as I sometimes get with her, she tells me that I'm the best mom in the world.

Though she is daddy's girl, she still gets very sad when I can't go to one of her hockey games or school events (I often work weekends).

She follows along with me when I beg her to hold my hand or to walk right beside me (though I try not to tell her that it's often because I'm freaked out).

Sometimes I tell her that I need a stick or broom or something to hold so that "I am able to walk" and she just passes it to me without saying that I'm insane. She thinks it's funny when I feel the need to go outside and yell, just to ease some stress… and she sometimes does it too.

I'm so glad for her awesome personality! She is carefree –I do not want to stop herspirit from running free through the skies.She is witty and smart and creative- she is a funny little fire cracker. She is insightful

We both share a love of books, of poetry and love of acting –she already does accents and role playing. We both like TV which sounds dumb, but we share some good time together watching cartoon 'Zorro' or 'Spirit'.

***

Those four astound me more and more every single day.

IF...

If the sun fell out of orbit,
And we never saw it again
The moon would be of no use to us either.
Without sunlight there is no moonlight,
Without you I won't shine
For you make me smile and you
Make me
Shine.

A MOANY TEST

I have heard that being saved is like wearing a parachute while you're on a plane. It's not comfortable and you probably look crazy. You probably wouldn't choose to wear one unless you thought you needed it.But when you need your parachute...

I like that that analogy doesn't make life seem like a Christian breeze, that it doesn't make Jesus just sound like a crutch. That analogy matches my life a bit.

I like being able to tell people that I know from experience that you can be imperfect in almost every way and still be Jesus'. I kind of think a story like mine helps a new Christian come out of the storm hand-still-in-hand with Jesus (being 'the seed that fell on good soil').

As hard as I've tried to run away, God's chased me down. As crappy as I feel, trying to go it alone does nothing but take away my peace.

John doesn't take away my pain by being with me. He does, though, comfort me a little bit by sitting on the couch while I scream and cry.

He does help me feel not alone. He does walk beside me in a parking lot so I'm not so scared. God is like that but 100x more. He *can* fix everything (bring hope). When He doesn't, it's for a purpose (also creates hope).

He gave Israel enemies so that He could see if they would really obey Him (and obedience is an act of love) (Judges 3:4). He gives us 'enemies' in the same way. Sometimes it looks a lot like abandoning us. In reality, it's because He loves us and wants us to grow in strength.

At the same time, He wants us to learn through adversity sometimes to trust Him and acknowledge that we need Him (is that an oxymoron? Well, God sometimes shatters what we think we know).

So when I realize that God isn't against me when I have adversity but is instead using it, I feel peace and trust. That what I go through can save a life. Like, really *save* them.

That when I've realized that God is with me *through* the pain rather than just a guy who takes away my pain, I actually feel kind of fulfilled; I actually feel like I have a purpose.

God is the one that has given me a huge promise that I can and do believe: He is creating an eternal home for me in heaven (John 14:2).

He wipes every tear from my eyes (Revelation 7:17). He has a good plan Israel (Jer. 29:11) and like them, He has one for me.

He is the God that came to give me life abundantly –because abundantly doesn't mean trial free, it means that you have hope and peace (John 10:10; John 16:33).

He gives the peace, even when your circumstances dictate other-wise (Philippians 4:7) He is the God that loves me fiercely and passionately.

He picks me up when I can't go on, on my own and He is with me through the storm. His are the arms that no matter what, I fall back into every single time because it feels too good to be with Him and too bad not to.

He is the God that died and rose again because He knew I'd come along at some point in time and He loved and loves me (John 3:16).

He knew that I was worth it, even before I deserved Him to save me (Romans 5:8).

He is the God that fights for me to give me the victory (Deut. 20:4). Yes, that doesn't always look like I want it to (ex: taking away my health issues!).

He will take me to Heaven because I can't do it myself. And why did I need saving so much anyway? Because I was separated from Him by sin.

God's nature can't abide with sin so without Jesus to sacrifice Himself, I'd remain sinful. And lost. God knew that many people would NOT accept Jesus' sacrifice but He sent Him anyway.

We just need to believe in Him and all that He did and is, and we can be with Him forever (have His Spirit with you while you're on Earth and go to be with Him in heaven at some point) (Romans 10:9).

How could you turn that down? I know I can't. I know that I'm too messed up to *not* realize that I need someone to tell me that they forgive my crazy (Romans 6:23), as many times as I do it.

So my testimony and witness of what God has done in my life is not all roses and rainbows and sunshine; in fact, it's mostly of clouds and storms.

But He was the one that brought me the rain when the ground was parched. He was the one that knew a negative Nelly like me doesn't appreciate rainbows all that much anyway.

All of my doubts in the past years have come from the father of lies, Satan (John 8:44). Everyone has the knowledge of God within them and I'm not different (Romans 1:20).

In times when I've felt really close to God I've prayed that He never lets me fall too far away, a little like King David's cry in Psalm 51:11.

If I can only give one testimony to God being real, that would probably be it. I prayed to God that He'd never abandon me and He hasn't.

Sure, He's let me go my own way when I really, really wanted to (ex: 2 Chronicles 15:2, He often leaves you to your own devices until the moment you come back to Him).

But He has never abandoned me and He'll never abandon you.

Bibliography

Hanegraaf, Hank (1993). What's wrong with the faith movement: part one: E.W. Kenyon and the 12 Apostles of another gospel. *Christian Research Journal*. 15(3). For further information or to subscribe to the *Christian Research Journal* go to http://www.equip.org

Lucado, Max (2007). *Every Day Deserves a Chance: Wake Up to the Gift of 24 Hours*. Nashville, TN: Thomas Nelson Publishers Inc.

Mattera, Joseph (September 19, 2013). *10 Ways the Word of Faith Movement Went Wrong*. Retrieved from **https://www.charismanews.com/opinion/41054-10-ways-the-word-of-faith-movement-went-wrong**. Charisma News.com.

Meyer, Joyce. Quotation. Retrieved April 8, 2019 from https://www.goodreads.com/quotes/57069-you-can-suffer-the-pain-of-change-or-suffer-remaining

Ten Boom, C. (May 21, 2015 by Debbie McDaniel). Crosswalk.com. Retrieved from **https://www.crosswalk.com/faith/spiritual-life/inspiring-quotes/**

40-powerful-quotes-from-corrie-ten-boom.html.
Copyright © 2019, Crosswalk.com. All rights reserved.
Article Images Copyright © JupiterImages Corporation.

Ten Boom, C. (November 1972 as cited in GUIDEPOSTS ONLINE). Retrieved from **https://www.guideposts.org/better-living/positive-living/guideposts-classics-corrie-ten-boom-on-forgiveness**.

Wieder, Dr. Lew & Gutierrez, Dr. Ben (2011). *Consider*. Virginia Beach, VA: Academx Publishing Inc.

Wikipedia. *"Word of Faith"*(2015). Retrieved from **https://en.wikipedia.org/wiki/Word_of_Faith**